The ISRAEL CONNECTION and AMERICAN JEWS

The ISRAEL CONNECTION and AMERICAN JEWS

David Mittelberg

Westport, Connecticut
London

DS
132
.M57
1999

Library of Congress Cataloging-in-Publication Data

Mittelberg, David.
   The Israel connection and American Jews / David Mittelberg.
      p.   cm.
   Includes bibliographical references and index.
   ISBN 0–275–96421–3 (alk. paper)
      1. Israel and the diaspora.   2. Jews—United States—Attitudes
   toward Israel—Statistics.   3. Jews—United States—Travel—Israel—
   Statistics.   4. Jews—United States—Identity—Statistics.
   I. Title.
   DS132.M57   1999
   305.892′4073—dc21   98–44401

British Library Cataloguing in Publication Data is available.

Library of Congress Catalog Card Number: 98–44401
ISBN: 0–275–96421–3

First published in 1999

Praeger Publishers, 88 Post Road West, Westport, CT 06881
An imprint of Greenwood Publishing Group, Inc.
www.praeger.com

Printed in the United States of America

The paper used in this book complies with the
Permanent Paper Standard issued by the National
Information Standards Organization (Z39.48–1984).

10 9 8 7 6 5 4 3 2 1

This book is dedicated to our children,
Yoel, Shuli, and Esti; to our nieces,
Tali and Liora; and to all the
children of Israel.
In their choices lies the Jewish future.

Contents

Figures

Preface

The context for this study is derived from two sources, the biographical and the intellectual. Within this context, I would like to relate to my reasons for writing this book? My decision to write this book is linked to my biography. In 1965 I was offered a scholarship for a year course in Israel called the Institute for Youth Leaders from Abroad. That year in Israel was critical in redefining the values of my Jewish commitment. I had long since left the Talmud Torah and had gone through a stage of rejection of traditional Orthodoxy, especially as it seemed to me in its archaic manifestations. It was not yet clear to me how being in Israel and being Jewish came together but in that year, in addition to studying Hebrew, I learned how I could be both modern and Jewish at the same time. At that point I think I probably decided that in one form or another I would resolve the tensions between being Jewish and modern in Israel and in kibbutz; the tensions between the religious and the secular, between Israel and the Diaspora, between the particular and the universal, between Yiddish and Hebrew. I returned to Australia after that year, accepted a senior role in the Habonim youth movement, and generally developed in that period a public profile as a Zionist activist within the Jewish community and a radical activist on campus.

On January 6, 1972 my wife Shoshana and I made aliya to Israel. We have three children who were born in Israel on Kibbutz Yizreel. From 1979 to 1980 I served as World General Secretary of Habonim, reimmersing myself in Zionist political life. I went from the more comfortable everyday work world of the kibbutz to accepting responsibility for the Jewish identity of young Jews, primarily those who had not yet come to Israel. Those were heady years in which I had my first insights into the nature of Israeli politics, the politics of the kibbutz movement, and Israeli society in general, primarily through the intensive relationship that I developed with the late Mussa Harif, at that time the General Secretary of the Ichud Hakvutzot VeKibbutzim Federation, and later to be a young and, unfortunately, short-lived member of Knesset.

In 1981 I read in the Israeli press of a forthcoming First World Gathering of Holocaust survivors which would include a conference for second generation Holocaust survivors in which I was invited to lead a workshop on the social and political implications of the Holocaust for second generation survivors. I wish to note two strong impressions with which I came away from that conference. I have since had the opportunity of confirming with other participants, especially Diaspora participants, that these were shared by others as well.

The first, which I cannot document scientifically, was a powerful feeling of commonality and commitment. The people who were there, hundreds of young people, were all about my age, looked similar, and spoke similar, although they were from all the four corners of the world. Many had been to Israel before on one youth program or another, and were articulate and sensitive to their own Jewishness and the issue of Jewish collective survival. In the room I felt a vibrant energy and a deep mutual identification between Jewish men and women, as well as a powerful sense of sharing which I felt could be, and ought to be, channeled towards positive, creative and innovative activities. But together with these feeling were also feelings of disappointment, alienation, miscommunication, and dissonance. This occurred when the plenum of second generation participants was addressed by an Israeli who made a well intentioned, but very unsuccessful address pleading for the immediate immigration to Israel of all the participants. She implied that their failure to do so was a rejection of their historic Jewish responsibilities. The speaker was a sabra, a native Israeli, and the audience was comprised mostly of Jews from the Diaspora. I felt a wide gap between the speaker and her audience. All around me I felt hostility rising and I thought to myself "Oh, God, you are losing them. This is no way to develop an Israel-Diaspora dialogue."

It was from this moment that I began to recognize a particular consciousness shared by the children of Holocaust survivors. I don't think this was by chance. This was the time when first and second born children of Holocaust survivors were becoming adults, bringing up children, and asking ourselves similar questions about Jewish continuity and survival, although now with adult sensitivities and directed to our children as opposed to ourselves. We ask not what have we become but what will become of our children and their future? And what of the future of the Jewish people to whom our children also belong?

What emerged for me, however, from the 1981 gathering of Holocaust survivors was the commitment to an Israel-Diaspora dialogue; an authentic search for a language of discovery and communication between Jews the world over. Yet as an Israeli, it seemed I had absolutely no way of furthering that goal. Israeli society appeared, and still appears, as sectarian and divisive, unable to generate the national leadership to clearly define contemporary Zionist goals, dominated by party politics and lacking in national consensus. It seemed unable to engage in a meaningful dialogue with world Jewry of my generation. This opportunity arose for me with the establishment of the Israel

Forum. Once again, fate had its role and by word of mouth I was invited to attend the founding meeting. I became active in one of the Forum's primary activities, which by that point had become one of my life's themes, namely, the bringing of Jewish youth to Israel.

The Israel Forum is a non-partisan coalition of Israelis from all walks of life whose mandate is to advance dialogue between Israeli and Diaspora Jews. The Israel Forum sponsors the Otzma Israel experience program in which young adult volunteers from North America spend approximately one year in Israel living on a kibbutz and volunteering in disadvantaged communities. I joined the lay committee that would organize that project. While I had no executive responsibilities, I felt it to be the natural place in which I could contribute what knowledge I had. After a year, Otzma began operations and is now in its 13th year. I have since been elected to the executive of the Israel Forum and been very active in its Israel-Diaspora dialogue along with the lay leadership of Otzma program. It has been and continues to be an exciting and inspiring personal and professional experience. I have come to feel for the first time that my Israeli commitment to being Jewish and my Jewish commitment to being Israeli are merging into a statement of purpose and a purpose of action. I am not sure at all what the final outcome of the Forum's activities will be. It has voluntarism as its keynote activity, and Israel-Diaspora relations as its mandate, which is another way of saying, dealing with the continuity and the future character of the Jewish people.

I also wish to address why this book focuses explicitly on the *"Israel Connection"* and American Jews. This is a particularly interesting question since in the last decade or so I have seen numerous demographic studies penned by prominent North American Jewish social scientists, all of whom are committed to professional excellence and Jewish continuity. They have visited Israel many times, both with and without their families, on academic sabbaticals, to participate in seminars, and for numerous other reasons. Yet, until very recently none of the major studies of American Jews dealt with the subject of this book in any way that is more than anecdotal. Although the spirit of these anecdotes anticipate some of the findings that follow here, these issues had never been systematically approached and analyzed. Why is this so?

The 1980s were characterized by a parochial euphoria on both sides of the Israel-Diaspora divide. Many Israelis felt Israel no longer had any need for the Diaspora, and many Diaspora Jews felt that their lives were in any way dependent upon Israel. The protagonists of this mutual distancing fed off of each other, reinforcing each other's attitude. The Diaspora openly rejected a Zionism based on immigration, or aliya, in favor of providing financial and political support. However, the purely philanthropic connection was just as alienating for the contributor as for the benefactor. The result was a patron-client relationship which was a far cry from a fruitful partnership. This sense of alienation was amplified by the gap between Israeli culture which is national and mostly secular and the culture of the American Diaspora which, at least historically, is based on the ritual and religion of synagogue life. In addition to this is the unfamiliarity and discomfort felt by many American Jews, the majority of whom are not Orthodox, with Israel's religious establishment and the political power it manifests. The Jewish Homeland, thus, did not feel quite at home for many of these committed Jews if and when they finally did visit Israel.

Jewish education, North American Jewry's primary vehicle for achieving Jewish continuity, has for the most part, been built upon a scattering of supplementary afternoon and Sunday schools. Ironically, voices emanating from the committed American Jewish intelligentsia were sorely critical of the generally negative impact made by this normative mode of American Jewish education. Jewish education seemed locked into a system that no one was happy with. A review of both popular and professional Jewish communal literature from the 1960s through the end of the 1980s often finds an Israel whose demands for aliya are mollified by political and financial support. Only recently has Israel been portrayed as a key resource for strengthening Jewish identification which might work to supplement, if not revitalize, what most recognized as an under enrolled and questionably effective Jewish education system.

By the same token, Israelis rarely considered what might be the positive contribution of Diaspora Jewry, qua Diaspora, to Jewish continuity *within* Israel. Israeli society, including the political establishment, tends to take the view that Jewish continuity in Israel is the outcome of demography and security, two internal issues to which Diaspora Jewry, by definition, cannot contribute directly.

It may be that today Israel is now ready to admit that it is top heavy with new immigrants, and that its future security and demography can be maintained even if American Jewry never resettles there. Israelis need to recognize that a dynamic and prosperous Diaspora community can engage and enhance Israeli society culturally, socially, and economically. At the same time, American Jewry must now recognize that Manhattan is not ancient Babylon and that Israel has a vital contribution to make to both the present and next generation of Diaspora Jews.

This study recognizes, a priori, the important contribution of both parts of the Jewish people to what has become the struggle for Jewish continuity. In this view Israel is not merely a geographic destination, but an ever present item on the American Jewish agenda. This is so with regard to: 1) personal, ethnic or collective identification, 2) social relations and networks, 3) economic partnerships, and 4) the development of Diaspora-Jewish institutional continuity.

This book examines the thesis that American Jews who have participated in an educational visit to Israel will do better on all empirical indicators of positive Jewish identity than those who have not. The Israel trip, it will be shown, is a unique experience that connects American Jews to their past, to Israel's present, and by virtue of its Jewish contribution to Israeli society and culture, to the future well-being of the Jewish people.

Acknowledgments

The empirical basis of this work is founded in large measure on the 1990 National Jewish Population Survey (NJPS), sponsored by the Council of Jewish Federations (CJF). While responsibility for this book lies solely with the author, there are many without whose help it would have been impossible to complete the project.

The data file and excellent documentation of the 1990 NJPS was made available to me by Dr. Barry Kosmin, Dr. Sidney Goldstein, Mr. Joseph Waksberg, Dr. Nava Lerner, Dr. Ariella Keysar, and Mr. Jeffrey Scheckner of the CJF and the Mandell Berman Institute-North American Jewish Data Bank, Center for Jewish Studies of the Graduate School of the City University of New York. Jeffrey Scheckner also made available the Statistical Package for Social Sciences (SPSSX) file of the New York 1991 Jewish Population Survey. Dr. Sergio Della Pergola and Uzi Rebhon facilitated the transfer of the NJPS SPSSX data file from the Hebrew University. Robert Ouzen, staff consultant at the Haifa University computer center, set up the SPSSX file that enabled speedy and efficient data processing. Motti Rimor generously answered my questions about data analysis and the NJPS file and variable definitions. Similarly, Dr. Steven M. Cohen of the Hebrew University and Dr. Steven Bayme, Director of the American Jewish Committee's (AJC) Institute on America Jewish-Israel Relations, offered important insights that helped clarify the methodological basis of this work. Parts of the data reported here appeared in an earlier AJC publication, "The Israel Visit." Permission to reprint this material is gratefully acknowledged. I am deeply indebted to my colleague and friend Professor Peter Medding, who read an earlier draft of some of the chapters of the book and offered challenging critical comments that eliminated flaws and enhanced its central arguments. Professors Barry Kosmin and Paul Ritterband read the entire manuscript at different stages of its development, offering important critical improvements both in style and substance. Dr. Sherry Israel of Brandeis University kindly provided me with the most recent data from the 1995 demographic study of the greater Boston Jewish community, which allowed important comparisons with the core data presented here. Others who read and offered helpful comments on one or several of the chapters included Roberta Bell-Kligler, executive director of Project Oren, and Professor Moshe Kerem.

I would like to record my especially deep indebtedness to Professor Sydney Goldstein of Brown University, who read the entire manuscript more than once, never tired of my inquiries, always responding graciously with important personal and scientific counsel, both of which were crucial to the conclusion of this enterprise.

The longitudinal data derived from the Otzma program is drawn from a now 13-year-long evaluation study, supported by consecutive annual grants by the Department of Education of the Jewish Agency for Israel. The wisdom, first, to make that undertaking when evaluation was not so popular, and second, to continue to maintain it for such an unprecedented length of time belongs to Martin Kraar, then the first CJF representative in Israel and thereafter the executive vice president of the Council of Jewish Federations. The data are published here with the permission of the CJF, JAFI and the Lay Leadership of the Israel Forum and North American Otzma Committees, the joint founding sponsors of the program. The sponsors and myself will be in agreement however, that the greatest thanks in this regard are due to the young men and women who participated in the program, gave of their time and energy both to its programmatic goals as well as to the completion of endless questionnaires throughout the program and even up to a decade after its completion. It is their volunteerism and commitment that have given inspiration to the writing of this book, credence to its findings, and offer hope to its readers.

This analysis was conducted at the Institute for Research of the Kibbutz at Haifa University. From an early stage, I received assistance with both NJPS and Otzma data analysis from my colleague at the Institute, Lilach Lev-Ari, for which I wish to record my long standing appreciation. In addition I wish to acknowledge the logistic and technical support offered by all my colleagues at the Institute but especially to Dr. Gila Adar the current director, Malka Miller, secretary, and Yaacov Glick, treasurer. I also wish to record my deep appreciation for the help of my research assistants, Betsy Winnick-Melamed and Andrea Cohen for assistance in analyses of the data and preparing countless drafts of research reports throughout the project.

I was most fortunate in having had the encouragement and support every author needs, from Dr. James T. Sabin, Director, Academic Research and Development at Greenwood Press, as well as the warm and meticulously intense support of Katie Chase, Project Editor, throughout all stages of the editorial process and production of the book. I am also indebted to Mr. Ardie Geldman, whose keen editorial work eliminated errors of syntax and style from the manuscript. Finally I wish acknowledge with gratitude a grant by the

Research Authority of Haifa University, which aided the preparation of this manuscript for publication, with special thanks to Angela Greenson who typed the tables and text in meticulous preparation for press, Yoel Mittelberg who prepared the illustrations and Adrea Megdell who diligently composed the index.

While the research was conducted at the Institute at Haifa University, I have served during this time as Chairman of Project Oren at Oranim, The School of Education of the Kibbutz Movement. My work at Oren for over a decade, has benefited immensely from the continuous support of a true friend of the kibbutz movement and especially of Project Oren, Mr. Morton Mandel of Cleveland. Mr Mandel has time and again by his personal example of community leadership, as well as through the generous support of the Mandel Foundation, raised the challenge to seek educational excellence scientifically evaluated, combined with programmatic vision spiritually inspired. I am therefore pleased to acknowledge with gratitude that this personal and Foundation support enabled me to continue to pursue both of these goals—neither at the expense of the other.

At the same time, I would like to thank all my colleagues at Oren who were willing so often to indulge my preoccupation with the completion of this task, carrying on at the same time the educational mission with which we were jointly charged. In particular, I wish to recognize Noami Meisels, the Executive Secretary of Oren since its foundation more than a decade ago, who always remains ready to ensure that I will be in a position to discharge all my many academic, executive and volunteer responsibilities always within the necessary time frame, doing so with professional excellence, personal commitment and a smile.

A man's home is his castle, Kibbutz Yizreel is indeed both home and castle. I wish to record my appreciation to my fellow members and lifelong friends on the Kibbutz as well as in the community at large, for providing that support which gives both substance and sustenance to life in a troubled land.

Finally, I wish to thank those who give particular warmth and meaning to life in any and every community—the family, my mother Leah Mittelberg and our children Yoel, Shuli and Esti, for their love and affection. It is my pleasure in more ways than one, to record here the depth of my most sincere gratitude to my wife Shoshana whose endless patience and warm personal support has been my most treasured resource for well over a quarter of a century. On our common journey, the completion of this book is but another milestone of shared accomplishment, a reflection—of that not so secret treasure.

CHAPTER 1

Introduction

This study analyzes the effect of a visit to Israel upon the ethnic identity of American Jews. For most American Jews, being Jewish carries both religious and ethnic connotations. The religious dimension is expressed on those occasions when ritual behavior is invoked, such as during life-cycle events both in the synagogue or home as well as on Jewish holidays or the sabbath. Otherwise, American Jews view themselves as one more ethnic group within the context of a multiethnic American society. It is because of this dual context, of both religion and ethnicity, that the Israel visit, which is the focus of this study, has a special significance for American Jews when compared, for example, to a visit to Italy for Americans of Italian descent, a visit to Ireland for Americans of Irish descent, or a visit to a black African country for African-Americans. The relationship of American Jews to Israel is bound up in the broader concept of *peoplehood*, a notion that encompasses a shared sense of religion, nationality, language, culture, and history.

The complex association between American Jews and Israel is better understood through an overview of the place of Israel and Zionism in the consciousness and lives of American Jews. Zion, one of the Biblical names for Jerusalem, has long symbolized an abstract religious ideal. Zionism, in contrast, refers to the nineteenth-century ideological and political movement that succeeded in reestablishing the first sovereign Jewish society in two thousand years. After the creation of the State of Israel in 1948, Zionism became, more than anything else, a vehicle for the preservation of Jewish identity. The historical background is followed by a theoretical discussion of identity, modernity and ethnicity, both in general, and in the American Jewish context. By examining the process of *migrant ethnogenesis*, the role of the *proximal host*, the meaning of *symbolic ethnicity*, and *community polity*, a sociological model emerges of Jewish identity in America.

The actual effect of the Israel visit on American Jews from different backgrounds and under various circumstances is analyzed on the basis of data taken chiefly from the Council of Jewish Federation's 1990 National Jewish Population Survey. The data from this landmark survey have yet to be analyzed for this purpose.

Findings from the NJPS are compared with three other sets of data. The first is taken from the 1991 New York Jewish Population Study (NYJPS), a major survey undertaken on behalf of the United Jewish Appeal Federation of Jewish Philanthropies of New York. Both the NJPS and the NYJPS employ a cross-sectional methodology—that is, they are based on survey data collected at one point in time from a random sample selected to represent a larger population at that time. Both these data sets were collected at the beginning of the decade. We will briefly also compare them with the most recent relevant findings drawn from the 1995 Boston CJP Demographic Study (Israel, 1997, 1998). The third data set is drawn from a survey of graduates of Otzma, a one-year community service and education program in Israel sponsored by the Israel Forum of the Council of Jewish Federations. The Otzma data are distinguished by the fact that they are longitudinal—that is, based on responses to survey questions administered over a period of time. Where the data of all three studies are compared, only the answers of respondents between the ages of 18 and 29 are used in order to allow a valid comparison of NJPS survey respondents with Otzma participants and alumni.

✗ A primary objective of this study is to present an accurate descriptive profile of those respondents who have never visited Israel, those who have done so only once, and those who do so frequently. This assessment includes attention to the social and demographic differences among them and what this implies for Jewish continuity. The Israel visit now has an almost urgent role on the American Jewish communal agenda. Recognizing the generally low level of formal Jewish education among American Jews and associating this with the reportedly high level of intermarriage (Goldstein, 1992), American Jewish leadership looks to the Israel visit as a key element for securing the Jewish future. For example, some Jewish organizations are considering providing one-time free airline vouchers to all American Jewish college-age youth so that each has the opportunity to visit Israel and it is hoped, undergo a positive Jewish experience that, among other things, would influence his or her criteria for choosing a marriage partner.

In this regard, the conclusions of this study may contribute to the policy planning process of Diaspora Jewish organizations currently involved in formulating strategies and allocating resources which will have an impact upon Jewish education and community survival. If the Israel visit is to develop into a key feature of Jewish communal life, the decision to finance the cost of this venture, even partially, will have to based on more than impressionistic data. This study offers its readers an opportunity to empirically examine the role the Israel visit has had in the lives of American Jews.

ISRAEL AND AMERICAN JEWRY

The connection between Israel and America's Jews has deep historical roots. The ideal of Israel, or Zion, has been present in the American Jewish psyche for over two hundred years. Documents which predate the American Revolution reveal how the Thirteen Colonies' nascent Jewish community, numbering only some 2,000, maintained a physical connection with the Holy Land (Karp, 1985:11). Mordecai Manuel-Noah, a well known figure in New York's Jewish community during the first half of the nineteenth century, considered the Jewish presence in America to be temporary. Since the Jews were there only until they could return to their homeland, he felt they should make it their priority to observe the Sabbath and to learn the Hebrew language.

The view that the Jews were a separate nation waiting for a physical return to the Land of Israel was emphatically rejected by most nineteenth-century American Reform rabbis. The leaders of Reform Judaism believed the essence of Judaism was "spiritual, not political or national" (Waxman, 1989:61). In 1898 the Union of American Hebrew Congregations firmly declared: "We are unalterably opposed to political Zionism. The Jews are not a nation, but a religious community" (61).

During the years 1880 to 1924 more than 2.5 million Jews from Eastern Europe immigrated to the United States (Feingold, 1974:120). Their different backgrounds led to two distinct views on Zionism. East European Jews did not distinguish between nationality and religion in the way that Jews from Germany and other West European countries did. The gradual integration of many first-generation East European immigrants and their children into the Reform movement made it possible for the movement to eventually accept Zionism during the 1930s. But the impressive growth of the American Zionist movement in America during the late nineteenth and early twentieth centuries did not reflect pure ideological commitment. Typically, Zionist organizations catered to many civic and social interests and aided new immigrants in their adjustment to American life. As a result, many American Jews became Zionists in name only.

In contrast to their Reform colleagues, almost all rabbis and lay leaders in the early years of the Conservative movement viewed Zionism as a legitimate, and even essential, element of Jewish belief. This is not surprising since Conservative Judaism was the product of a transplanted East European Jewry. However, the Zionism of American Conservative Jews was different from the earlier European version. European Zionists upheld the notion of *shlilat hagolah*, the fundamental rejection of the Diaspora as a home for the Jewish people. Conservative leaders of American Zionism, on the other hand, saw a reborn homeland in Palestine as the "spiritual center" of the Jewish people which would inspire and strengthen Jewish life throughout the Diaspora. This essential ideological difference continues to echo today among those engaged in the "Israel-Diaspora dialogue."

CULTURAL ZIONISM IN AMERICA

Beginning as far back as Israel's prestate period, but especially since June 1967 when the Jewish state won a seemingly miraculous victory in a defensive war which threatened to annihilate it, many American Jews have both followed and played a role in developments in Israel. Their devotion to and support of local institutions, whether the Jewish National Fund, hospitals, homes for the aged, rabbinical seminaries (yeshivot), or entire new communities became reason enough to call themselves Zionists. What came to be known as "cultural Zionism" arose, ironically, in response to the movement's growing success. As Jewish settlement in Palestine continued to develop, supporters in America sought a way to qualify the Zionist precept to "live in the Land." American cultural Zionists supported, both spiritually and financially, the immigration to Palestine of Jews from throughout the world, but could not accept the obligation to move there themselves.

Rabbi Mordecai Kaplan (1881-1983) an early leader of Conservative Judaism, saw in Zionism "the cultural regeneration of the Jewish people" (Waxman, 1989:71). Kaplan identified with the writings of Achad Ha'am (the pseudonym chosen by Asher Ginsberg, 1856-1927), who had a profound effect on the development of Zionist thought during the late nineteenth and early twentieth centuries. Kaplan was initially opposed to the secular political Zionism of the modern movement's founder, Hungarian born, Austrian citizen Theodore Herzl. Kaplan did not think that Zionism in America should promote emigration. He believed it was unrealistic to expect Jews in the West, particularly in the United States, to leave a country in which they felt so much at home. He did not, however, think it unreasonable for the Jewish people to contribute to the creation of a Jewish homeland for those seeking refuge from persecution. Kaplan wrote, "Zionism as a movement to bring about the spiritual or religious revival of all Jews throughout the world would be fully entitled to ask the Jewish communities of the free countries to provide their quota of able-bodied and high charactered men and women to come to Israel either to live there permanently or, *at least, to devote several years to its service*" (Waxman, 1989:71, my emphasis). Kaplan, it appears, was one of the first to recognize the role of Israel in hosting Jewish visitors from throughout the world.

The influential American Jewish Zionist, Judah Magnes (1877-1948), was an ordained Reform rabbi who turned to Conservative Judaism in his later years. After a long and illustrious career on the pulpit, Magnes moved his family to Palestine in 1922, where he became the first president of the newly established the Hebrew University. Nonetheless, he, like Kaplan, did not view aliya, as the *sine qua non* of Zionist commitment. And like Kaplan, he was drawn to the cultural Zionism of Achad Ha'am, whom he called "The Harmonious Jew." Magnes's Zionist credentials were unassailable, but his more flexible approach helped to legitimate the American Jewish model.

In contrast to their East European-born fathers and grandfathers for whom identification with the fate of the Jewish people was the core of their existence, Jews in America developed a more circumscribed and individualized ethnoreligious identity. This development no doubt affected their attitude toward Zionism. "American Jews [during the first half of the century] were, by and large, totally uninterested and unreceptive to a Zionism which was based on nationalism, because they [no longer defined] themselves as a national group but, rather, as a religious one" (Waxman, 1989:75).

While Zionism that emphasized nationalism was generally not of interest, spiritual Zionism was considered both legitimate and praiseworthy. American Supreme Court Justice Louis Brandeis (1856-1941), a major figure in early American Zionism, emphasized the complementary nature of American and Zionist values. He felt that the assimilation and disappearance of America's Jews into the surrounding society could not be avoided unless "there be established in the fatherland a center from which the Jewish spirit may radiate and give to the Jews scattered throughout the world that inspiration which springs from the memories of a great past and the hope of a great future" (*Encyclopedia Judaica*, 4:1297). Yet Brandeis also dismissed the obligation for American Jews, in particular, to move to Israel. American Zionist activity, thought Brandeis, should concentrate on building Jewish settlement in Palestine for needy immigrants from other countries.

The search for spirit, inspiration, and Jewish pride, more than culture, was what really animated the "cultural Zionism" of American Zionists. Culturally, they remained Americans through and through. Their allegiance to America and its values was so great that only a relatively few American Zionists evinced the motivation for learning Hebrew. This language deficit, perhaps more than any other factor, served as an obstacle to developing an insider's understanding of Israeli life. The physical distance which separates Israel and the United States symbolizes the cultural rift between Israelis and American Jews. It is in this context, as we shall later see, that the Israel visit plays a special role.

LABOR ZIONISM IN AMERICA

As the name implies, "Labor Zionism" is different from "Cultural Zionism." The Labor Zionist movement in America began in 1904 as a working-class effort whose primary goals were the abolishment of capitalism and the bringing of young Jews to Palestine to "join in the practical work of redeeming the land" (Goldberg and King, 1993:35). To this end, it established youth groups in America primarily populated by young Eastern European immigrants raised with the socialist idealism of the Old Country. As this movement grew, its members interest in socialism became overshadowed by an emphasis on Zionism. Officially Labor Zionism remains loyal to the tenet of aliya, although over the years it became clear that one could remain active in the movement without a commitment to settling in Israel.

Labor Zionism appealed mainly to the young. Hechalutz, literally "the pioneer," was the name of a Labor Zionist organization that was founded in 1905 to encourage young Jews to settle in Palestine. After the Balfour Declaration in 1917, whereby Britain declared its support for the Zionist cause, a large contingent from Hechalutz enlisted in the British army's Jewish Legion to fight in Palestine. The movement dissolved more than a decade later when a new American Hechalutz organization was formed that served primarily as an educational and training ground for those with a commitment to live in Palestine.

In the 1920s another attempt was made to attract American Jewish youth to Palestine when a new organization, Young Poale Zion (the Young Workers of Zion) was formed. This name was later changed to Habonim (the Builders). The organization was also committed to the struggle against assimilation and to the education of Jewish youth. When the Arab riots broke out in 1929 the Young Poale Zion directed all its energies to defending the *chalutzim,* or young Jewish pioneers, in Palestine. In 1947, in the months leading up to Israel's declaration of statehood, Labor Zionist groups mobilized Jewish youth in America to offer their skills in establishing settlements in Israel and fighting for independence. The immediate prestate period saw the largest number of North American Habonim settlements established in Israel.

The creation of the State of Israel served as a watershed for Labor Zionism. The movement had witnessed its primary objective fulfilled and was now challenged with redefining its goals or falling into obsolescence. The leaders of Habonim quickly realized that despite the dramatic developments in Israel, American Jewish youth were either ignorant of or indifferent to the whole subject. In response, Habonim created a workshop and a training camp which provided young Jewish adults the opportunity to see Israel by touring, living, working, and studying on a moshav or a kibbutz (two forms of collectivist communities).

The impact of the Labor Zionist movement on the American Jewish youth it did succeed in involving was significant. Although it no longer urges living in Israel, for over four decades the movement has given young Jewish adults from the Diaspora the chance to see and experience Israel through intensive educational and work study programs. As a result the movement has turned out dedicated and capable leaders, including many rabbis and educators. While it never succeeded in capturing the interest of the masses, American Labor Zionism continues to play an active role in American Zionist circles. Still, its future may be called into question as Israel itself moves further away from socialist ideology.

THE CENTRALITY OF ISRAEL IN AMERICAN JEWISH LIFE

While Political Zionism has little practical meaning to American Jews, Israel is present in their lives and helps to give meaning to American Jewish identity. Even if they are not Zionists according to the classic definition, most American

Jews are pro-Israel. They support Israel "politically, economically, emotionally" (Waxman, 1989:108). It has even been asserted that "the pro-Israel sentiment of America's Jews is part of the attempt to fill the gap of modern homelessness" (115), a theme to which we will shortly return. The role of the Israel visit in strengthening emotional attachment to Israel is illustrated by the Otzma findings discussed below.

Philanthropic support for Israel continues to be the primary means through which American Jewry expresses its involvement in the Jewish state. The United Jewish Appeal, established in 1934, symbolically unites the American Jewish community through a massive fund-raising effort on Israel's behalf. This organization is responsible for one of the top three most effective annual nationwide fund-raising campaigns in the United States. One of the most successful fund-raising methods to be developed by the UJA is the Israel mission, a fund-raising version of the Israel visit. Silberman (1985) describes the role of the mission as a means by which a select but small proportion of the American Jewish community express their commitment to Israel and bring meaning and expression to their lives as Jews in America. The missions allow participants to meet with high-level Israeli politicians, listen to a "confidential" briefing on Israeli's security, and visit an army or air force base, giving participants a sense of being on the inside of what is happening in Israel. Missions usually also focus on Israel's role as a "haven for persecuted Jews while reminding the visitors of the continuing threats to its security" (Silberman, 1985:198). Participants visit Yad Vashem, Israel's national memorial to the Holocaust, immigrant absorption centers, and settlement towns that are populated by new immigrants. The last night of the mission is usually devoted to "card calling," when the mission participants are asked to pledge money. The spiritual debt to Israel is thus redeemed while the Jewish identity of the Diaspora Jew is simultaneously enriched.

While the UJA collects money exclusively for overseas purposes, primarily Israel, the New York-based Council of Jewish Federations, acts as a national umbrella organization for all local Jewish federations. Federations are involved locally and regionally in community planning, policy making, and helping to provide social and educational services for Jews. Through fund-raising, community organization, health and welfare planning, public relations, and leadership development, local federations offer many opportunities for communal involvement. In today's American Jewish community, it is through their local federations that many Jews maintain at least some connection with Israel. The high public profile and broad-based involvement of the federations, on international and national issues, sectarian and nonsectarian, act as a vehicle for Jewish unity. This also indicates to non-Jews that the Jews of America value their Jewish identity.

The federation movement developed into a major force in Jewish communal life in the post-1967 period. Israel's Six-Day War was a watershed for American Jews who suddenly found themselves publicly expressing concern for their ethnicity. Prior to this experience many American Jews sought to "melt" into the American mainstream. Since that time, federations, in cooperation with the UJA, have committed themselves to ensuring the growth and survival of American Jewry by focusing on the unity of the Jewish people, with the State of Israel as its central symbol, or "spiritual center."

The increase in the number of federation and other communal leaders visiting Israel in the last decade is an indication of how many Jewish organizations seek to uphold this symbol and keep Israel near the top of their agenda. In 1983, among the board members of major national Jewish organizations, 94 percent had visited Israel at least once, while 78 percent had visited two or more times (Silberman, 1985:200). In contrast, the purely symbolic value of Israel to most American Jews is reflected by the somewhere less than 30 percent who have ever visited there (see Table 14).[1]

Woocher (1986:67) refers to the way in which Americans express their identity and faith as Jews through their activism in the Jewish community as "Civic Judaism." The work of the federation movement is consistent with the core beliefs of Civic Judaism. The major tenets of Civic Judaism are Jewish survival and the unity of the Jewish people, the centrality of Israel, a tie to tradition, a commitment to pluralism, equality and justice, and the provision of social welfare, or the giving of charity. Any activity that promotes these principles strengthens the Jewish community and unites the Jewish people everywhere.

PILGRIMAGE AND TRAVEL TO ISRAEL

The tradition of visiting Israel for Jews has historical connections dating back to the First and Second Commonwealths. As prescribed by the Torah, Jews made pilgrimages to Jerusalem three times a year on the festivals of Passover, Shavuot, and Sukkot. Following the destruction of the Second Temple in Jerusalem by the Romans in 70 CE and the dispersion of the population, pious Jews continued to visit the Holy Land, although the once joyous journey was now marked by sorrow. Throughout the exile that followed, the desire for redemption through the return of the Jewish people to its land became established as a central theme in Jewish liturgy and texts.

Israel's importance to Judaism, Christianity, and Islam and the fact that it serves as a natural land bridge connecting Europe, Asia, and Africa, promoted pilgrimage throughout the centuries. One of the earliest recorded impressions of Israel by a Jewish traveler was documented by Benjamin of Tudela. He arrived in the Holy Land as a tourist and recorded his experiences for the period 1159 to 1173. His motivations for travel to Israel seem to have been a mixture of commerce and religious pilgrimage. His point of departure was Spain, and he documents his travels through Europe, the Holy Land, and the Middle East, but especially Jerusalem. Jerusalem was at that time under the control of the Crusaders. He describes a city of about 1,500 Jewish families and an equal number of Samaritans. Indeed, wherever he traveled he described the geography and demography of the Jewish communities he encountered. His description of the holy sites in Jerusalem constitutes the forerunner of the modern travelogue.

CONTEMPORARY TRAVEL TO ISRAEL

It was not until the beginning of the eighteenth century that people traveled solely for pleasure. Prior to this period, tourism was primarily for economic or religious purposes: trading goods or making religious pilgrimages. The European "Grand Tour," viewed as both a holiday and an educational experience, became a popular form of travel in the eighteenth century for wealthy young people, although the greater part of the tourist industry was government-subsidized trips mainly for the purpose of exploration and expanding trade. Medical reasons were another popular motivation among eighteenth- and nineteenth-century "tourists." Samuel Pepys documents the popularity of "medicinal spa water" and sea bathing for the curing of ailments (Bull, 1991:17).

The idea of mass tourism began to develop as a consequence of the industrial revolutions, which meant new and cheaper means of transport including the steam railroad and the steamship; a rise in personal income; work benefits which provided vacation time and the desire for escape from the filthy and crowded urban landscape. Furthermore, economic development brought with it the desire to visit friends and relatives. An increase in labor mobility meant the breakup of families. Thus, family reunions created a significant travel need. To this day, visiting friends and family makes up a large part of international tourism.

Today, mass tourism for purposes of recreation is a major segment of world tourism, with aircraft replacing the train and steamship as the popular mode of travel for large groups. In addition, new technology and unlimited advertising have brought about the rise of "supply-led" tourism, whereby the tourism suppliers introduce and market a specific tourism product (Bull, 1991:17).

Israel has a unique attraction to foreign tourists. Visitors to Israel may be differentiated according to their motivations for and expectations of their visit, as well as according to the different ways in which they choose to explore the country. Some visitors come for a purely recreational holiday, some for an educational experience, some to see the biblical sites, some to visit relatives or friends. Others come on organized missions focusing on different themes. Above all, Israel is "The Holy Land," the cradle of Judaism, Christianity, and the location of Islam's third holiest city, Jerusalem. Israel's historical holy sites draw more people than any natural or man-made attractions. Still, the modern State of Israel has created other reasons for both short- and long-term visits, primarily in the areas of commerce and education. Its Western-style economy is based on modern industry and high technology. Its universities attract researchers and students in all fields from throughout the world. Since the end of the Gulf War in 1992 and the beginning of the Middle-East peace process, the number of tourists visiting Israel has increased. A record number of 2.2 million visitors entered the country in 1994. Clearly, Israel is becoming a more popular place to visit.

Figure 1
Israel Experience Youth Programs Based on World Participation, 1966-1993

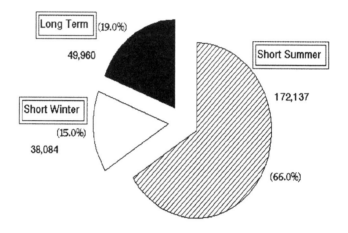

HISTORY OF MODERN VOLUNTEERING IN ISRAEL

In addition to the reasons cited above, travel to Israel has for many thousands of people centered around a volunteer experience. There are many reasons why a person might choose to volunteer in Israel. Often this decision is influenced by external factors affecting Israel, such as politics, the prospects for peace, and the issue of security. Voluntarism, as a form of, or precursor to, the Israel visit, is documented at least as far back as Israel's 1948 War of Independence when the many Jewish, but also non-Jewish, *Machal* (volunteers from abroad) risked their lives in battle and served on the home front. Voluntarism was again sparked by the labor shortage in the country during the time of the 1967 Six-Day War when nearly 7,500 young Jews from around the world came to offer their services.

Volunteering on a kibbutz has for many years been a popular way many non-Jews and Jews from around the world get to experience Israel. Kibbutz volunteers share certain motivations, such as a desire to participate in and observe the unique kibbutz lifestyle, to see Israel in a manner that is relatively inexpensive, and, often, as one leg of a worldwide itinerary.

Voluntarism still continues today, although the experience has undergone a severe process of institutionalization and routinization. Israel's Kibbutz Program Center in New York City was established in the late 1970s in order to coordinate the recruitment of volunteers for work on kibbutzim (plural), as well as to recruit volunteers for short-term summer programs, educational tours, year-long work-study programs, among many volunteer opportunities.

In addition to it being of interest to non-Jewish pilgrims, tourists, business people, and academicians, Israel plays a special role as the destination each year for thousands of Jewish youth from around the world. In this capacity Israel fulfills a special function, for unlike any other country or homeland in the world, visits to Israel are used by Jewish parents and educators as a framework for instilling Jewish knowledge and strengthening Jewish identity. According to the Statistical Abstract of Israel (Della Pergola and Rebhun, 1994), from 1967 through 1993 there were 6,918,725 visits to Israel from the United States and 746,427 from Canada. Dr. Eric Cohen cites an undocumented source which estimates that since the 1967 Six-Day War "approximately half a million Jewish youngsters (have come) to Israel," including all types of volunteers (Cohen, 1993:2). Dr. David Harman, the director-general of the Jewish Agency's Joint Authority for Jewish Zionist Education, estimates that more than a quarter of a million Jewish youth from around the world have participated in educational programs and organized trips in the last two decades (Harman, 1993:6). These data, which have been collated and presented in detail in Figure 1, represent a radical departure from the pre-Six-Day War period, when the numbers of Jews (adults or youth) visiting Israel were substantially less. The numbers of youth who have visited Israel in the framework of the Jewish Agency from 1966 to 1993 are indicative of the scale of the enterprise.

NOTE

1. All tables are at the end of the book.

CHAPTER 2

The Visit to Israel

PREVIOUS RESEARCH

In June 1984, Jewish communal leaders and educators from 31 countries met at the First World Leadership Conference on Jewish Education in Jerusalem. The conference affirmed that Jewish identity was in crisis and that increased Jewish education was the appropriate response to that crisis. It also affirmed that what was labeled "the Israel Experience," an educational encounter with Israel and Judaism directed toward Jewish teens and college-age adults, was a central means by which Diaspora Jewish education could be enriched on a large scale, both in quality and in scope.

Subsequently, the Jewish Agency's Board of Governors created a special Jewish Education Committee chaired by lay leader Morton L. Mandel of Cleveland, which in turn set up a subcommittee on the Israel Experience led by Robert Loup of Denver. In March 1985, Annette Hochstein, director of Nativ, a private Jerusalem educational research institute, was commissioned by the Jewish Education Committee to undertake a comprehensive study of Israel programs currently offered, examining their effectiveness and their potential for the future.

WHO VISITS

As noted earlier, between the years 1966 and 1993, just over a quarter of a million Jewish youngsters from all over the world participated in some type of educational program in Israel under the auspices of the Jewish Agency. Sixty-six percent of these participants came for a short summer visit, while the remainder came for a full semester or one-year program. The fluctuation in the level of participation in these programs over the years mirrors the historical patterns of war and peace in the region, such as the exhilaration of victory in 1967 and 1973 and the trepidation of the years of Lebanon, the Intifada, and the Gulf War.

In 1966, the baseline for these data, a total of only 3,500 Jewish youngsters came to Israel from all over the world compared to over 7,000 only one year later. However, while in 1967 just under one-half of these participants came in long-term programs, by 1977, a decade later, the peak year of the entire period under review with over 13,000 participants, only 15 percent were long-term visitors. By 1988 the global number of participants had dropped to about 7,000, rising again in 1993 when it stood at 9,591 of whom only 20 percent were long-term, mostly college-age participants (Table 1).

The two decades of the 1970s and the 1980s each brought the same total number of participants, around 102,000. The peak period was between 1976 and 1987 when over 10,000 participants per annum arrived in Israel. The exceptions were 1980 and 1982. When comparing the decade of the 1970s to the 1990s, we notice a comparatively higher number of participants in Israel youth programs throughout the 1970s as compared to the 1990s. A principal reason for the drop in participants in the 1990s is a decline in the size of the 18-24 age cohort as illustrated in the data from the 1971 National Jewish Population Survey (Massarik and Chenkin, 1973:271; and Della Pergola, 1972:3). On the basis of these data, we can estimate that the 18-24 age group numbered 13 percent of the core Jewish population of 5,420,000 in 1971 or approximately 704,600 individuals. Whereas in the 1990s, this same age cohort represents 9.5 percent of the core Jewish population of 5,515,000, which equals approximately 489,250, a decline of 33 percent. An additional factor that may help to explain the decline in participants is the growing number of participants brought to Israel outside of the Jewish Agency framework by federations, Jewish community centers, and synagogues. Nevertheless, it can be assumed that the general trends reflected above were repeated with these and other program purveyors.

What percentage of these participants came to Israel from North America? It is difficult to compare Jewish Agency worldwide data and those representing just North America collected by the Charles R. Bronfman Foundation (CRB) because of the likelihood of overlapping cases (Table 2A). A reasonable assessment would have it that around 60 percent of all youth participants in Israel programs came from North America. This follows from the assumption that about 20 percent of the participants reported in the CRB data are not represented in Jewish Agency global data, although, again, this is only an estimate. What is clear, nonetheless, is the small representation of college-age participants. In 1992 there were only 1,006 college-age participants of whom more than half were in long-term nonuniversity programs (Table 2b), the remainder were in short-term nonuniversity programs. The 1990s therefore reflect the strange situation where emphasis on the Israel Experience as a means for strengthening Jewish identity has so far realized a lower rate of participation in Israel youth programs than took place in the late 1970s without the communal emphasis.

In June 1986, Annette Hochstein (1986) submitted to the Jewish Agency Jewish Education Committee her summary report on educational programs in Israel. Hochstein's first-ever, comprehensive database catalogue of Israel programs established that there were then some 400 different Israel educational programs in which, in 1985, 41,500 individuals participated. The study divided them into three main categories: 19,000 participants in informal programs and study; 15,000 participants in formal educational institutions such as yeshiva, high school, and university; and 7,600 participants in work or other volunteer programs. Sixty percent of the participants were between the ages of 18 and 30.

A market study commissioned around the same time by Hochstein, on behalf of the Jewish Education Committee and conducted by Professor Steven Cohen (1986), estimated that the Jews in the United States could be divided roughly into three parts: one-third who had been to Israel, one-third who had never been but wished to, and one-third who had never been nor wanted to come. In contrast, almost three-quarters of the Jewish community of Melbourne, Australia, had visited Israel at least once. Among American Jews, those who had already visited Israel showed some religious observance and shared certain other characteristics such as a strong Zionist commitment, some degree of formal Jewish education, and a high degree of communal affiliation.

The one-third who had never been to Israel but would like to visit had weaker affiliate links with the Jewish community; for example, they may have belonged to a Jewish institution but were not active in it. Most had received some form of part-time Jewish education and their religious affiliation was equally divided among Conservative or Reform Judaism, and being "just Jewish." This group did, however, have the benefit of a social network of family and friends who had visited Israel and were able to provide information and enhance motivation.

Respondents in the Cohen survey who had little or no interest in visiting Israel were characterized by a lack of involvement in Jewish life. This segment of the population was identified as having no formal Jewish education, little or no communal affiliation, and a low rate of ritual observance. Indeed, as Cohen noted "[it is their counterparts] the heavily involved [who] are already being effectively recruited to Israel programs" (Cohen, 1986:11).

DOES VISITING ISRAEL HAVE ANY IMPACT ON JEWISH IDENTIFICATION?

The effect of an Israel visit on measurements of Jewish identity is approachable in two ways. The first method is through community or nationwide studies (Mittelberg, 1992), where cross-sectional data derived from a given population are analyzed to assess the strength of the correlation. The second is through direct program evaluation, where the impact of a specific program, or programs, is evaluated by their participants and others (Mittelberg, 1988). While there are significant differences between these two methodologies, the findings arrived at utilizing both indicate that a visit to Israel is positively associated with and/or responsible for an increase in measurements of Jewish identity. The ideal study would require longitudinal data in order to measure characteristics before and after an Israel visit occurred, as well as a comparison of these same measures with a control group that did not visit Israel at all. What we are able to do here is use the NJPS parallel age cohort as a surrogate control group in a comparison with the longitudinal data of Otzma.

The impact upon participants of one Israel program has been reported in detail by Mittelberg (1988). The Kibbutz Ulpan program was identified early on as a setting in which considerable impact on Jewish identification measures could be achieved provided the experience was qualitatively high. Indeed, Cohen's study identified up to 10 percent of 18-24 year olds as being interested in visiting Israel as a kibbutz volunteer.

In the spring of 1990, a conference at the Project for Kibbutz Studies at Harvard University entitled "Innovation and Evaluation of the Israel and Kibbutz Experience of North American Jewish Youth" (Mittelberg, 1990) convened more than 50 leading scholars in the fields of sociology and education, from the United States, Canada, and Israel. It dealt with the major issues of the role of Israel in the Jewish identity of North American Jewry and the impact that a visit to Israel, and particularly to a kibbutz, has on this identity. At that conference, Cohen, in a paper entitled "The Impact of Israel Travel upon Jewish Identification," reported on his analysis of cross-sectional data from a 1989 study of the American Jewish community. The analysis compared levels of selected indicators of Jewish identification for those adults who had never been to Israel with those who had visited once or more. The results indicated that Israel travel does not account for the frequency with which Jewish holidays are observed but has a somewhat larger correlation to measures of communal affiliation (e.g., belonging to an organization or synagogue). Where Israel travel has a small to moderate correlation, its weight seemed to be greater than that which can be attributed to any major type of Jewish schooling. At the same conference, Sternberg and Rimor (1990), found additional support for this in a smaller sample of Hillel student leaders.

At that same conference a paper by Mittelberg (1990) entitled "Longitudinal Evaluation of the Israel Experience: The Case of the Kibbutz Institutes for Jewish Experience" offered a comprehensive model that included the major qualitative elements of the kibbutz experience: staff, social integration with kibbutz members, accommodations, and satisfaction with the educational program. The latter included seminar centers, sites visited, and kibbutz educational programs, all of which were outlined and evaluated. All of the components in the model were found to affect the degree to which the Israel Experience enhanced the participants' sense of Jewish fulfillment at the conclusion of the program (Mittelberg and Lev Ari, 1991). Additional papers presented at the conference that included different age groups and employed both longitudinal as well as cross-sectional methodologies also noted the ability of a variety of programs to have a positive influence upon Diaspora participants (Kafka and London, 1990; Urman, 1990; and Shulman, 1990).

Using data from the 1985 Boston Jewish community survey, Mittelberg (1992) demonstrated the independent contribution of the Israel visit toward measures of religious practice and community affiliation beyond that made by Jewish schooling. In the same paper, this relationship is also discussed within the context of a longitudinal analysis of the Project Otzma Israel experience program, though here the time frame extended only from beginning to the end of program and not beyond. Utilizing data from the most recent work in the field, the 1995 Boston Community survey, Sherry Israel has demonstrated the "added value" of an educational trip to Israel on adult measures of religious practices, as well as organizational and philanthropic behavior (Israel, 1998:100-102).

S.M. Cohen (1991b) in an unpublished paper on Canadian Jewish youth, examined the impact of visits to Israel on an index of Israel attachment. His findings confirm his earlier work, that visitors are more affiliated than non visitors, but more important, that one visit seems to have only a limited impact when compared to two. Particularly useful is the strategy employed by Cohen for this assessment, which compares the scores on "Israel attachment" between "intenders" who have never been to Israel and "once only visitors." For the sake of comparison, this strategy assumes that "intenders" are similar to "one-time visitors" in their pre-trip Jewish and demographic characteristics so that attitudinal differences between them can be attributed with some confidence to the impact of the visit itself. The findings in this book are similar to Cohen's, albeit with different emphases.

Chazan (1997) has prepared an updated and comprehensive analysis of over 100 items of recently reported research, investigating the impact of the Israel experience on identity formation among youth visiting Israel, where he identifies three causal models of how this impact may be generated. The *domino* theory implies that the Israel visit is a serial threshold in a life plan that leads to other additional experiences that have educational consequences; the *cluster* theory asserts that the Israel experience in parallel with other experiences together produce an educational impact in concert, while the third theory attributes to the Israel visit an *independent* causal weight of its own. Overall, this research gives weight to the view that the youth visit to Israel has outcomes for measures of Jewish identity in adulthood. It does so because it affords the opportunity for experiential learning within and about Jewish time and space, within a peer culture which entails positive Jewish self-esteem and appropriate role models.

Yet this same research leaves Chazan with a considerable number of unanswered questions beyond the routine consideration of the weight of ideological content as well as pedagogical excellence on the program outcome.

First, are the measured effects in adulthood, in large part a reflection of the self-selection of program participants, the critical factor of who goes to Israel or what happens there? Second, is there a more or less propitious age for visiting Israel that optimizes the behavioral consequences of that visit? Is it during high school, college, or perhaps even later? Third, to what degree is the measured impact on adult behavior a function of the Israel visit itself or the postvisit environment and programming? These issues will be addressed in what follows.

The final question was not raised by Chazan at all—namely, to what extent is the perceived impact of the Israel visit a reflection of a real phenomenon rather than a reflection of the instrument of measurement? Indeed most of the authors reviewed are careful to place serious caveats around their findings to limit claims of causality or predictability. This scientific modesty notwithstanding, it is still worthwhile to point out that while in cross-sectional studies causal inference is limited seriously because of a lack of time order of events, these studies do have the advantage of representing large populations, indeed entire communities, so they cannot be ignored. At the same time, among the program evaluations there are important methodological differences between their evaluation strategies. Among these we find those that engage in retrospective evaluation at the end of a program only, those that engage in retrospective evaluation of alumni only (years after the conclusion of the program back in North America). Others, seeking a higher degree of causal inference, engage in pre/post longitudinal analysis from the beginning of the program to its conclusion in Israel; while finally a few isolated programs have engaged in true longitudinal analysis that includes pre post and then follow-up analysis on the very same respondents, on identical measures of Jewish identity, years later in the country of origin North America.

The problem, however, is that the question that Chazan rightly raised— namely the role of self-selection of participants and thereafter respondents—is found at all of the stages of program recruitment, implementation, and then evaluation, so extreme caution must be always exercised in interpreting evaluation. By way of illustration, it is sometimes argued that college-age participants are those most impacted by an Israel visit and that this is because of the generally longer duration of their program. Erik Cohen (1998), in a post hoc summative evaluation study, informs us that among participants in Israeli university overseas programs 75 percent had been to Israel before, 86 percent had a parent who had visited. At the same time, Mittelberg and Lev-Ari (1995) report that among participants in the Oren program who are also college age, 46 percent had never been to Israel before the program. The Oren study thus gives both the educators and the evaluators an opportunity to gauge the impact of a single educational experience in Israel on measures of Jewish ethnicity among adult alumni of the program. The principal findings were that the experience served as a transformative agent of participant's ethnic identity, independently and cumulatively to the formative role of home background and Jewish schooling. Thus for Oren alumni, being Jewish became a central part of their lives in terms of their degree of religious practice, the density of their ethnic social ties, and the intensity of their connection with modern Israel.

In the chapters that follow it will be important to build both on the substantive as well as the methodological lessons of the research briefly reported thus far—both to elucidate the differential role of the Israel visit in the biography of its participants through long-term research, as well as to seek clues for general extrapolation of these findings through comparison with nationwide and communitywide studies. In both fields caution, albeit of different kinds, will be properly applied.

CHAPTER 3

Identity, Modernity, and Ethnicity in the Cross-Cultural Encounter

SOCIETY AND IDENTITY

In this chapter we analyze the relationship between modernity, ethnicity, and identity in order to clarify the issues that make up the discussion of Jewish continuity. By examining the processes of migrant ethnogenesis—namely, the dynamic of identity formation following migration, the role of the proximal host, the concepts of symbolic ethnicity, community, and polity—we can begin to understand the wider social context in which ethnic identity, and Jewish identity specifically, develops and is nurtured.

For Berger and Luckman (1967), society is an on-going dialectical relationship between the individual and the social environment. The human world is a world of culture, yet since it is a human product that must continuously be recreated, it is inherently precarious and open to change. Jewish identity in modern society is a matter of subjective choice. Culture derives its objectivity by virtue of its being both external to consciousness as well as collectively recognized as real and shared by fellow humans. The modern Diaspora Jew is compelled to recreate his or her own Jewish order within the non-Jewish world in which he or she lives.

Berger raises the question of the relation of human meaning to social structure in his concept of the *Nomos*. In Greek *Nomos* means law. Berger, however, derived the term by inverting Durkheim's *anomie* (normlessness or social alienation). In many ways *Nomos* carries the meaning of the opposite of anomie. To understand what Berger means by *Nomos* we must keep in mind his notion of the *social construction of reality*. For Berger, "the . . . socially constructed world is . . . an ordering of experience. Meaningful order, or

Nomos, is imposed upon the discrete experiences and meanings of individuals" (Berger, 1967:19).

The maintenance of the constructed subjective reality is realized by our continuous conversation with significant others (peers, parents, etc.), so that each person's socially constructed world "requires a social base for its continuing existence as a world that is real to actual human beings. This base may be called its 'plausibility structure'" (Berger, 1967:45). That is to say, the education of collective values and their perpetuation requires a community to generate and maintain their reality status. Continuity can then never be an idea, only a consequence. The maintenance of such a plausibility structure is more difficult for an ethnic group in pluralistic competition with the values of a wider society than where the entire society shares one set of values.

MODERNITY AND IDENTITY

Berger and Luckman's theory of society outlined above, with its emphasis on the *Nomos*, or order, as the constituting principle of "One's Life World," lays the foundation for Berger's later view (Berger et al., 1973) of modern society as being characterized by a pluralization of life worlds. When Berger et al. speak about modernization they refer to "the institutional concomitants of technologically-induced economic growth" (9), the primary ones being technological production on the one hand and bureaucracy on the other. In contrast to premodern society where all aspects of one's life world were integrated through a symbolic universe, modern men and women typically live in a plurality of life worlds, each with its own symbolic universe where the primary overall integrating mechanism is the individual's own criterion and typical migration between these worlds. This pluralization of life worlds is revealed in the daily migration between private life and the world of large public institutions. While the former is home, the latter is not. Modern individuals are not "at home" in a great part of their daily life. Now, it is only the private world that provides an individual with a *Nomos* of integrated and sustained meaning, so that the *Nomos* is no longer coterminus and perhaps not consistent with the whole of the larger society in which one lives.

Indeed, while this pluralization may engender a "sophistication" to strangeness, it also at the same time weakens the plausibility structure of the home world itself. More systematically, the pluralization of social life worlds manifests itself in a syndrome consisting of two interrelated components. The first component lies in the possibility of alternate career plans or biographies of the individual. One needs to make decisions, project one's life, taste both the freedom of choice and of frustration. Modern men and women can engage in rational and rationalized anticipatory socialization as to what "they will be when they grow up."

The second related component Berger et al. call "multi-relational synchronization" (68). Here a person organizes the multiplicity of social relations and their respective plurality of careers, together with their concomitant institutional referents and empirical timetables. Together, these two components comprise the syndrome of modern life called the lifeplan. The lifeplan is both technical coordination of all the above time-tables and possibilities, as well as their meaningful integration. It is both a value and an end in itself in modern society. Indeed, Berger's view of identity (Berger et al 1973:73-74) is specifically modern in four ways, which can be summarized as follows:

First, it is open in the sense in that all adult socialization is incomplete, making the modern always conversion-prone. The possibility of being other than what I am today is endemic to modern life.

Second, modern identity is differentiated. It is derived from a social world that is pluralized, weak in its internal coherence and stability, and in its ability to act as an overall meaningful referent. Thus, the reality status of the world derives primarily from the subjective experience of self rather than the objective realm of social institutions.

Third, this predominance of experience of self together with the need for constant career planning and decision making makes modern identity particularly reflective. It is through reflection that the lifeplan is constituted so that identity and social life acquires the subjective meaning which in premodern society was mediated directly with the overall meanings inherent in the integrated objective institutions.

Finally, and consequently, modern identity is individuated, that is to say, the contemporary political philosophy of liberalism or the rights and freedom of the individual's life are rooted in pretheoretical consciousness itself derived from modern social structure.

If, for Berger et al., religion provided men with the ability to be "at home" in the cosmos, pluralization with its secularization gives rise to the modern feeling of homelessness and brings in its wake ongoing attempts by men and women to recreate this meaning, which for Berger et al. is anthropologically necessary, or at least optimal.

The study reported here gives special attention to contemporary American Jewish young adults. In this perspective they are necessarily seen as "conversion prone," where personal ethnic identity is endemically open, residing in an ever-secularized world of pluralized meanings. Here subjective meaning is endowed by virtue of the act of individual choice exercised formatively, typically during maturation and young adulthood.

If the demodernizing impulse lies at the heart of modern societies, it has the effect of homelessness, so that the yearning for demodernization is the quest for being at home in contemporary society. For the young modern Jew this may well be a double quest involving both a national-ethnic home as well as a private one. In this view, the demodernizing impulse becomes the structural source of the ethnic revival of the 1960s with its celebration of cultural pluralism, while the particularistic content of ethnicity of each and every ethnic group is considered as a micro consequence, rather than a macro cause of the phenomenon.

Almost 30 years ago Berger recognized the special difficulties of Jewish social existence in the Western world. He correctly identified that its problem "manifests itself more significantly in the disintegration of religious practice" (Berger, 1967:169), rather than in doctrine. However in a perceptive anticipation of the ensuing debates, both on American as well as Jewish ethnicity, Berger (169-170) observed that

> the peculiarity of Judaism as a religious tradition and an ethnic identity means that the problem of its plausibility, *ipso facto*, entails what is referred to as the "crisis of Jewish identity." The Zionist attempt to redefine Jewishness in terms of national identity thus has the ambivalent character of, on the one hand, re-establishing an objective plausibility structure for Jewish existence while, on the other hand, putting in question the claim of religious Judaism to being the *raison d'etre* of Jewish existence.

These issues of demodernization, cultural pluralism, and modernity all have important significance for an understanding of contemporary American Jewish identity and the cultural setting within which the visit to Israel takes place. In order to understand the struggle for Jewish continuity and changes that have taken place in Jewish identity, one must first examine the larger picture of ethnicity in America. Ethnic revival is understood in these terms as an attempt at the attribution of meaning in modern pluralized society, a framework in which Diaspora Jews feel particularly comfortable. Paracommunity in an individuated and individualistic society lends itself easily to what has been termed recently as the "partial community of shared individual feelings" (Medding et al., 1992) within the contemporary segmented ethnicity of American Jews.

ETHNICITY AND JEWISH CONTINUITY

The existence and ongoing nature of ethnic groups has been studied from both macro and micro approaches. Consistent with Mittelberg and Waters (1992), these two approaches are used to define ethnic identification and examine the point at which the two approaches converge to create a definition of ethnic identity. In the macro approach theorists have looked at the historical and geographical determination of ethnic groups, the content of cultures and traits which comprise the group, and the nature of power relations in societies which put one or another group in a position higher or lower in the hierarchy. The micro approach has been concerned with the dynamics of ethnic identity and identification, with the process of boundary maintenance and movement across boundaries, and with the question of how individuals make decisions about the salience of their ethnicity to them, about which of various ethnic options they will choose in their own identities, and about whether to invoke ethnicity and ethnic identities in political mobilizations and everyday personal encounters.

The study of Jewish ethnicity in North America has been limited largely to analyses that derive from the second approach, whether implicit or explicit. Jewish ethnicity is often written about as if no other ethnic groups existed in North America. Furthermore, the literature does not sufficiently emphasize the fact that ethnic continuity is determined just as much by the dynamics of the wider society as by internal developments within the ethnic group along any or all of the otherwise well-documented behavioral indices of Jewishness. Yet neither ethnic continuity nor its negative measure, outmarriage, can be even conceived let alone analyzed outside a theoretical framework that systematically accounts for the wider society on all those same dimensions being considered within the ethnic group. This study will attempt to offer a more comprehensive inclusive and typological approach to ethnicity in general and Jewish ethnicity in particular, one that includes the macro categories of ethnicity of the wider society of which it is a part.

This typology can be illustrated by way of an analogy with the formative experience of the emergent ethnicity of migrants to North America, an analogy which in its substantive content is not foreign to almost all of the ethnic groups in contemporary America. However, it is not this genetic historical fact that makes the analogy so relevant but rather, it is argued here, that migrant ethnogenesis is the analogue of ethnic continuity—the latter is the former routinized. This is so, it seems, because ethnic identity, and consequently its continuity, is dynamically in flux as is the wider society itself, indeed as are the cultural determinants of the latter that make ethnicity at all possible. Some clear examples of these categories might be American cultural pluralism and its emergent multiculturalism, the vagaries of the economy and its consequences for class differences and social mobility as they are expressed in variables of educational attainment and income. All of this generates a marriage market that becomes in the open society a major agent for social mobility for large numbers of white ethnics located in certain identifiable strata of American society, *inter alia*, Jews of the middle class. What then is migrant ethnogenesis and what is the typology of ethnicity on which it is based?

MIGRANT ETHNOGENESIS: THE PROXIMAL HOST MODEL

Here, following Mittelberg and Waters (1992), we identify three social actors involved in the dynamic of identity formation following migration. Two are familiar to theories on this subject and one is a relatively new addition. First, there is the individual immigrant. He or she uses elements to determine his or her own identity and also to attach a positive or negative valence to that identity. Second, there is society at large, which uses elements to determine the immigrant identity and also to attach a positive or negative valence to that identity. Finally, there is also the collection of people called the "proximal host"—the group to which the receiving society would assign the immigrant— it being the waiting category in the minds of the individuals in the receiving society. In other words the proximal host is the group that the wider society would define as the immigrants' coethnics. In this view the outcome of the immigrant's identity will be a result of the assignment by the receiving society, the cognitive map of the immigrant themselves, and the conceptions of the proximal hosts—the ethnic group to which the individual immigrant would be assigned.

The typology of ethnogenesis proposed here includes the dimensions or building blocks of ethnicity of the groups and the different interpretations and reactions to those dimensions among the different aspects of the host society and the society of origin. The dimensions of ethnicity include race, religion, shared history and origins, language, nationality, and class.

In the United States the kinds of ethnic categories in place range widely in terms of their consequences for the individuals classified in each of the categories, in terms of the range of choice allowed to individuals in how to classify themselves and in terms of the strategies or agendas adopted by the different groups. The spectrum or typology of types of ethnicity in the United States is presented in Figure 2 (Mittleberg and Waters, 1992:417). The groups are arranged along a continuum from left to right of (1) a lesser to a greater degree of influence of ethnicity on individual behavior, and (2) the degree

Figure 2
Spectrum of Types of Ethnicity in the United States

Individual Choice--Societal Constraint

Unhyphenated	Symbolic	Ethnics	Migrants	Language	Race
Whites	Ethnics			Minority	Minority

of choice of ethnicity open to individuals. In the United States, as race and shared origin are the axes most determinative of ethnic identity, it is those groups which are defined racially who have the least amount of options or flexibility for changing into other types of groups.

Unhyphenated whites are one end of the spectrum. This group, descended from primarily the North and West European early immigrants to the United States, especially from England, no longer claim a particular shared history and origin. They do not think of themselves as a category but define themselves as American on surveys and censuses. (For a more detailed description of this population, see Lieberson, 1985.) In the next category are symbolic ethnics, who identify with a shared history and origin and a nationality such as Irish-American or Italian-American. However, there is a lot of choice involved in the particular categories the people choose to invoke. The groups have no organizational basis and it is only in terms of affective ties and leisure voluntary activities that they display their ethnic identities. (For a detailed description of symbolic ethnics, see Waters, 1990.)

In the next category are ethnic groups. These groups have an ethnic identity which does not hinder their full participation in American society but which has more than just a symbolic component to it. For instance, their ethnic identity still influences their choice of marriage partners to some degree. Generally there is an organizational component to these groups in that there is some corporate entity or concrete group to which the individual belongs. American Jews who are members of organizations or synagogues would be classified as an ethnic group.

The next more intrusive type of ethnic identity we call immigrant. This is an identity which is still a very salient and intrusive identity in terms of national loyalty, everyday life, and feeling apart from the host society. In general, immigrant people are composed of groups with a high degree of separation from the host society. In terms of residential dispersion or concentration, for example, they are likely to live either in ethnic ghettos or rural communities. While the tendency historically in the United States is that these groupings survive only in the first generation and then change to more assimilated ethnic groups and symbolic ethnic groups in future generations, there are exceptions to this rule such as the Amish who have managed to maintain a very separate way of life for many generations, in spite of the lack of wider societal discrimination. Haredi (ultra-orthodox) Jews in New York may provide a similar example of such separation in the Jewish community.

The final two groups are labeled as minorities, on the basis of Wirth's definition: "a group of people distinguished by physical or cultural characteristics subject to different and unequal treatment by the society in which they live and who regard themselves as victims of collective discrimination" (Stone, 1985:42). One can distinguish among groups defined by language—Hispanic groups in the United States—and those defined by race, such as Afro-Americans. First-generation migrant Jews to North America once belonged to this category. However, in the past three to four generations they have moved away from the category of minority group and may now often be defined as symbolic ethnics. Minority groups are the least integrated into the wider society and have the least amount of choice in terms of self-identification.

Ethnicity involves ways of thinking, feeling, and acting that constitute the essence of culture. Ethnic patterns must be related to the larger social matrix in which they are embedded. Ethnicity is dynamic, the outcome of the negotiation of a collective identity at the interface between two cultures in the biography of ethnics, lived through the history of their communities. In short, the ethnicity of any group cannot be derived exclusively either from the macro categories of the wider society or to the restricted micro cultural domain of the group itself. Rather, it is necessary to analyze the reciprocal relationship between the two in order to delineate the different theoretical and empirical options that are open to every ethnic group. It is the empirical options of Jewish ethnicity and ethnic Jews that we will now examine.

ON THE MEANING OF BEING JEWISH IN AMERICA TODAY

Both Medding et al. (1992) and S.M. Cohen (1991a), like most scholars and popular commentators, have discussed in depth the ongoing debate between "optimists" and "pessimists" concerning the future of American Jews. The pessimists predict the disappearance of a distinctive Jewish community, seeing only the survival of the Orthodox. Those who are more optimistic perceive a "transformation" and even revitalization of the American Jewish community. Rising rates of intermarriage provide an opportunity to strengthen the ranks of American Jewry through an infusion of new blood or "imports"—the born non-Jewish spouses and their children. (Medding et al., 1992:3) This metasaga has raged for so long and continues to do so only because it has been matched with a concomitant lack of clarity and/or consensus about what it means to be Jewish and thus to know when one has ceased to be one.

This debate is not recounted here. However, there is a difference in the approaches of Cohen and Medding et al. Their most recent thoughts represent diverging theoretical viewpoints on the subject of this section. Whereas Cohen presents a bifurcated typology that sees the development of two sorts of Jews, the federation versus the synagogue, Medding et al. offer us a segmented one that reminds us that the Jews, as do all moderns, make their own typology. Indeed, there are in fact infinite choices available including the denial of being other than Jewish or non-Jewish in what Medding et al. call "dual identity" households. In Cohen's terms the Jewish world seems to be a zero sum storehouse of Jewish culture, more of one type (federation Judaism) might mean less of another (synagogue Judaism). Medding et al. tell us that if the world is at all zero sum then it firmly includes the non-Jewish world, through its non-Jewish spouses and the dominant non-Jewish culture in which Jewish ethnicity lives and breathes, which in turn generates all the ethnic options open to contemporary fourth-generation American Jews.

Cohen's work actually presents a fascinating mosaic of forms of Jewish life in America. It is rich in presentation and detail and its description seems to catch the moment very well. The problem lies with the typology and the cautiously optimistic extrapolations which it allows, which may in part be due to a too literal reading of its formulation which is encapsulated in the title of his research report "Content or Continuity? Alternative Bases for Commitment"

(1991a). In this typology content is defined as "dedication to a particular brand of Jewish culture and community, such as Orthodoxy, Conservatism, Reform, secularism, political liberalism, or Zionism". Cohen discusses the well-known denominational differences and cleavages on a whole range of behavioral and attitudinal measures of Jewish life, from holiday observance to organizational membership. As he and others have shown before, Orthodox respondents outscore Conservative respondents, who in turn outscore the Reform. What then is continuity?

Cohen describes continuity as "passion for Jewish survival in any recognizable form, be it a particular denominational style, merely sentimental, or otherwise" (5). Commitment to Jewish continuity can be measured in several ways, through membership in a synagogue, involvement in a community activity, communal affiliation, having Jewish friends or living in a Jewish community, subscribing to Jewish periodicals, belonging to a cultural Jewish organization, contributing to the Jewish Federation or UJA, or maintaining close ties with friends or family living in Israel.

The misleading element here is not in the distinction between content and continuity, but in their presentation as logical sociological alternatives. Since the hierarchy of affiliation which Cohen proposes is in any event structured accordingly, the activists who are at the top of this vertical linear continuum yearn for content (denominational and religiously based) and, of course, continuity. The middle segment of Jews (50 percent), while found to have lower scores of religiosity, affirms its Jewishness proudly and is left with "continuity." At the bottom end of the scale are the marginally affiliated and often outmarried who yearn, it seems, for neither. Therefore, this is not an alternative typology at all, but a two-stage monotonic linear continuum, at the base of which lies the fact that many Jews today do not think being Jewish requires religious observance even though one may belong to a synagogue.

SEGMENTED ETHNICITY

Medding et al. (1992) offer a major theoretical innovation by recognizing the dynamic change in contemporary Jewish ethnicity. In their terminology, the change of Jewish ethnicity has been from "a community of belief" to a "community of shared individual feelings," from a normative community to an affective one. The community of belief constitutes "a total system that controlled the individual's environment with a detailed pattern of prescribed actions and fixed roles" (17). In contradistinction, contemporary Jewish ethnicity, they observe, is characterized as a "voluntary and partial community of personal choice with unclear boundaries and undefined membership" (17).

What stands at the core of this Jewishness is not a high degree of Jewish ritual practice but rather a high or low degree of group belonging, affect and pride, together with an unambiguous rejection, of the dominant Christian culture. Thus Jewish continuity means, on the one hand, belonging to the

Jewish group and, on the other, not belonging to the Christian one. Yet Medding et al. refer also to a partial community of individual feelings. This partiality is a function of choice which is selectively articulated at rites of passage such as birth, marriage, and death. Thus Jews can choose what segments of Jewish community are salient, meaningful, and powerful for them and are not compelled to take all or nothing. These segments include "religion," "culture," "philanthropy," and "Israel." This typology allows for subjects to choose which segments they do or do not at all include in their repertoire of Jewishness and what degree of valence or intensity they attribute to each and every one of them.

The Jewishness of the "community of shared feelings" is segmented in a number of ways. First, it is but part of a more comprehensive identity, and second, echoing Berger's analysis of the structure of American identity per se, the "multiple aspects of identity coexist independently, rather than coalescing to form a larger integrated whole . . . [resulting] in a pluralistic personality" (Medding et al., 1992:18). Thus the Jewish segment may have many components or few, such as religious practice, affiliation, and the like, while the intensity of any one or all of these components may vary differentially. Despite this multiple segmentation, at its core contemporary Jewishness is unambiguous about one thing—it is not Christian. Whether the identity is weak or ambivalent, it is "Jewish and nothing else" (19).

Medding et al. utilize this typology mainly for the study of outmarriage (in far greater depth than will be done here). The thrust of the argument is that this pluralized, individuated mode of Jewish ethnicity allows for or is open to the empirically rare option of affirming an intense Jewish identity while engaging in nonconversionary outmarriage. For it is the shared ethos of American liberalism and American ethnicity that allows both partners, Jewish and non-Jewish, to enter the marriage with a view that the heritage of neither is at stake. Whether the separate elements of this blended ethnicity can be sustained in the second generation and beyond, or are bound to become a terminal option as Medding et al. argue, is a major issue of concern which is beyond the scope of this book, but will be briefly alluded to later. It will be argued that the Israel visit serves to increase the salience, valence, and meaning of whatever Jewish identity segments respondents adopt as well as providing an additional segment for their identity repertoire, both public and private.

In addition to the typology itself, Medding et al. makes two more claims with respect to Jewish ethnicity and outmarriage that will be considered here. The first is the role of Jewish education; the second, the weight of socioeconomic factors in determining Jewish behavior. With respect to the former it is claimed that there is a relationship between Jewish education and rates of inmarriage. Where these differences are "based on duration of Jewish education, particularly so in younger age groups . . . the association between more than six years of Jewish education and inmarriage is stronger in younger age groups" (12). With respect to the latter, it is argued counterintuitively that the lower and not the higher socioeconomic status is associated with higher rates of outmarriage. Both of these arguments will be examined later within the context of the NJPS data to determine their relative weight in molding the relationship between the Israel visit and all other measures of Jewish identity.

In summary, Jewish ethnicity according to Medding et al. is characterized by the following components: (1) personal choice, (2) affect and not belief, (3) segmentation and not integration, and (4) an unambiguous core that is non-Christian. What they find is an increasing number of dual-identity households, since outmarriage no longer entails the surrender of Jewishness or the abandonment of its continuity, but the transformation of the meaning of being Jewish itself.

The view of identity as an outcome of the encounter with non-Jewish society is echoed in a recent paper by historian Arnold Eisen, whose views of modernity reflect, at least in part, those of Peter Berger. In Eisen's words, for Jews "modernity has been negotiated primarily in terms of practice and not in terms of belief. The key has been rituals performed and reinvented, comments heeded, ignored and reconfigured, communities fragmented but still operative, authorities subverted, but still potent" (Eisen, 1994: 2).

Eisen proposes a set of five bases of Jewish authority in contemporary American Jewish society: (1) socially constructed reality, (2) religious experience, (3) meaning symbols of family and community life, (4) community per se, and (5) ancestors. His conclusion offers us the following reflection on modern American Jewish identity. "Our selves are hopelessly divided. The integration we manage to achieve is hyphenated, and we will *never simply be Jewish alone*" (Eisen, 1994: 11, emphasis added.) Fortunately, in the absence of a competing exclusionary ideology in the West, Eisen is able to console himself with the words "modernity need not destroy us and will in no way save us" (Eisen, 1994: 13).

Eisen has indicated elsewhere (1992), however, the emerging role that Israel may acquire in helping to shape Jewish identity in North America, though he points out the problematic nature of the traditional mode of attachment to the State of Israel in the identity of contemporary American Jews (Eisen, 1992: 9-12). He offers alternative strategies for restructuring that attachment in order to maintain a new but positive role as a salient segment of American Jewish ethnic identity. Eisen presents five modes of "improved interactions" between Diaspora Jews and the State of Israel. These include people-to-people interaction through (1) visits to Israel, (2) home hospitality, (3) joint projects, (4) community twinning arrangements, and (5) traditional philanthropy, as well as demands on American Jews to become better learned in Jewish and Israeli culture and the Hebrew language. The extent to which these strategies are operable may delineate the future character of evolving American Jewish ethnicity, community, and identity.

SYMBOLIC ETHNICITY AND AMERICAN JEWS

Waxman (1981), accepts Herbert Gans's theoretical definition of symbolic ethnicity as that which identifies later-generation whites who share a common history, origin, and nationality and who freely choose to express their ethnic identity. Indeed, He cites sociologists who, in the 1960s projected a "trend of accelerated cultural and to a lesser degree, structural assimilation (which) would lead to what Milton Gordon refers to as 'identificational assimilation', the loss of identification with the ethnic group" (83).

However, Waxman challenged this projection, arguing that American Jews are undergoing an ethnic revitalization of intrinsic Jewish cultural patterns in the following: Jewish schools, increased ritual practices as well as a pro Israel stance (84). Indeed, "most American Jews define the survival and well-being of Israel as sine qua non for the survival of Jewry" (79).

This latter faith in the civic ethnicity of pro-Israelism has been challenged in recent years. However, work by Steven Cohen (1991) indicates, in fact, that the apparent erosion in attachment to Israel of younger-generation American Jews has been arrested. Thus while in 1989, 34 percent of those under 40 expressed a high attachment for Israel, by 1991, after the Gulf War, this rate rose to 47 percent. In addition, in the same period, the gap between old and young narrowed rather than widened, largely as a result of a considerable increase in the degree of attachment among younger adults and a stability in attachment among older adults (38). Thus, Israel serves as a major source of affect for being Jewish in America.

More recently, Kivisto and Nefzger (1993) also identify symbolic ethnicity as a variant of straight line assimilation theory. They also categorically reject Gans's typology and teleology. However they identify symbolic ethnicity as the response to the survey question, "How important is being Jewish to you?" They find, not surprisingly, that Jews who regard being Jewish as important also maintain Jewish religious practices and affiliative ties with the Jewish community. This is a tautological and obvious treatment of the concept. Such Jews are not symbolic ethnics; they are clearly ethnic Jews. Thus, this presentation neither addresses nor refutes our concerns. Here, we defined symbolic ethnicity quite differently. It signifies the limiting case—namely, when respondents are Jewish and something else, rather than Jewish and nothing else.

In rejecting Gans's prediction of ethnic assimilation, Kivisto and Nefzger argue for Jewish exceptionalism on the grounds that Jews are a religioethnic group. In their last sentence they argue for the persistence of their definition of symbolic ethnicity, following Sanford Lyman, on additional grounds of identifying another force which is characterized by an incommunicable ineffability "appreciating the remarkable tenacity of ethnic identities in a contemporary world perhaps begins with a recognition of its irrational and mysterious wellspring" (10). This form of reductionism is a priori empirically irrefutable in the Popperian sense and hardly useful for analysis. Fortunately there seem to be more prosaic explanations for persistence of symbolic ethnicity even when properly and more narrowly defined, as will be seen.

The question is not, after all, whether mainstream American Jews should be regarded as symbolic ethnics, and if so, whether this condition must inevitably lead to assimilation, but rather whether we are witnessing the emergence of a new variant on a broad continuum of Jewish expression—that is, in the mode of symbolic ethnicity. If this is occurring, what are its parameters, why does it persist, will it indeed lead to assimilation or to anything at all?

Gans has rejected the criticism of Kivisto and Nefzger (1993) having recently updated his concept of symbolic ethnicity with the parallel concept of symbolic religiosity. Symbolic religiosity, which develops, in his view, primarily among immigrants and their descendants, refers to a "form of religiosity detached from religious affiliation and observance" (Gans, H., 1994:578) in which the "consumption of religious symbols, apart from regular participation in a religious culture and religious affiliations—other than for purely secular purposes" (585).

Gans illustrates his theory by citing previous analyses of American Jewry (Cohen, S.M., 1988). As both the data Gans cites as well as the data in this study show, American Jews have shown an increasing preference for celebrating Jewish holidays, particularly Passover, that are based in the home rather than in the synagogue. This "home-centered religion" allows people to honor religious holidays without the formal constraints and demands made by rabbis or by the surrounding religious community. Indeed, when those who attend a home-centered celebration such as a Passover seder feel that it intensifies their Jewish identification, it serves as a perfect exemplification of symbolic religiosity.

Modern American Jewish ethnicity, whether characterized as segmented or symbolic, is regarded as problematic for those charged with the task of Jewish education and Jewish continuity in America. Jonathan Woocher (1994a) reports an attenuation of Jewish identity among Jews in America today which he attributes primarily to the voluntary nature of Jewish identity. In his view, while most American Jews are in no way ashamed of their Jewish ethnicity, the salience or importance attributed to their Jewishness has declined significantly. As a result, Judaism moves to the periphery of self-identification, no longer providing significance or meaning to daily life, asserting itself only at particular moments in biography such as rites of passage, or when the possibility of marrying a non-Jew arises. Why is this so?

In line with our earlier discussions on ethnicity, modernity, and identity, Woocher raises questions relating to what ought to be the goals of the contemporary Jewish community. Indeed, what ought to be the new basis for the Jewish community that is currently at risk or that has been lost? Woocher, too, recognizes the element of personal choice in the voluntaristic element of ethnic continuity and ascribes the loss of community to macro forces within society, cautioning against reducing the problem of Jewish community to being merely a question of personal choice of yea or nay. In Woocher's words, reflecting both the "pluralization" of Berger and the "segmentation" of Medding, Jewish identity has become:

1. Hyphenated, i.e., existing alongside other group identities in an individual's self-definition.
2. Fragmented, i.e., broken up into components affecting specific areas of an individual's cognitive, affective, and behavioral life-space, but without integrating these as a whole.
3. Truncated, i.e., not impacting certain areas of the life-space which are, therefore, effectively devoid of Jewish influence.
4. Pluralized, i.e., found in many variations which may or may not be or regard themselves as compatible with other variations.
5. Marginalized, i.e., operative primarily in areas distant from the core of self definition.
6. Homogenized, i.e., blended with elements of other identities so as to reduce its distinctiveness (Woocher, 1994a:16).

The importance of this definition lies in the fact that it goes beyond Woocher's earlier groundbreaking definition of the organizational and ideological basis of the civil religion of Jewish community. In his view, the only way to transform the Jewish identity of individuals and make it a larger part of one's self-identification is to create a coherent and effective plausibility structure which will take over where the existing Jewish community has fallen short. The contemporary American Jewish community is characterized by a lack of unity and strength making it a weak social structure for the enhancement of Jewish identity. Woocher's solution to the fragmentation of the institutional structure of the Jewish community is the creation of an overarching plausibility structure which will require existing institutions to work in unison with shared aims. The focus should be "the social and behavioral bases for Jewish involvement . . . which will invite attachment and subsequently provide ideological legitimization for that attachment" (Woocher 1994b:15).

Israeli society, and the kibbutz as a particular example, as functioning Jewish communities, may provide a highly effective "plausibility structure" for the transmission of Jewish values and likewise the enhancement of Jewish identity. The power of Israel lies in the fact that it is exactly what the Diaspora is not. Nonetheless, while Israeli society provides the ideal community for exposing Diaspora Jews to a wholly Jewish society and culture, hence increasing the salience of Jewish identity, the challenge lies in maintaining this strengthened Jewish identity after returning home where Jewish plausibility structures are weak. What is required in Woocher's view is the prior existence of a real Jewish community for Jewish education to be effective, the absence of which in North America he laments. He calls for the creation of a "living Jewish community in which what is being taught and learned is already visible and valued," thus making Jewish education thoroughly "enculturating" rather than instructional (Woocher 1994b:25).

While Woocher acknowledges the impact of various educational experiences such as day schools, summer camps, youth group programs, and trips to Israel, he argues that their impact often declines fairly rapidly once the individual is removed from the supportive social environment created (Woocher, 1994b:26). At least part of this claim will be challenged later—namely, the rapid dissipation of the long-term impact of the Israel experience after the participants have returned home to their country of origin. This challenge is brought in the context of our analysis of the longitudinal data on participants in the Otzma program.

Woocher raises the issue of Jewish community as a Durkheimian moral, or normative imperative, in its role of constituting the plausibility structure for American Jewish life. It is, in fact, a sine qua non for Jewish education and continuity. This community is located in the public institutional domain where it is necessary to enhance the basis of individual attachment and individual and collective behavior. This position requires an analysis of the current bases of mobilization of personal involvement into American Jewish institutional and communal life, to which we now turn.

CHAPTER 4

Behind the Symbols: Community, Polity, and American Jewish Ethnicity

THE NATURE OF AMERICAN JEWISH ETHNICITY

Michael Gross (1993) analyzes American Jewish ethnicity through the dichotomous contrast between (1) primordial or organic ethnicity, which stresses ethnic persistence and particularism, and (2) organizational ethnicity, which emphasizes political integration through the development of voluntary association (5). This dilemma emerges from his view that "there are competing claims of ethnicity and multi-culturalism" (6-7). While he is correct in distinguishing between these dimensions, regarding each as an independent variable, he appears to understate the degree that they are also interdependent and thus should not be seen as mutually exclusive or competing.

Gross's important contribution lies in his presentation of the organizational paradigm which "defines an ethnic group primarily in terms of the integrity of its voluntary associations" (26), which he contrasts with the organic paradigm where "[t]he integrity of the ethnic group [is] measured by the absolute number of members and the preservation of the very primordial ties which define the group: language, shared history, other cultural artifacts, and lineage" (9).

Gross uses this definition pejoratively, since it is seen as particularistic and antithetically opposed to the goal of integration while engendering a "hierarchically arranged and ethnically segmented social order" (Ibid.). It is interesting that Gross first discusses the social structural segmentation of ethnic groups and not the segmentation of the subjective identity of social actors. Whether one overlaps the other is not clear here. Second, it unnecessarily, perhaps, links hierarchy and segmentation, talking the language of power, although not explicitly. Gross does not even raise the possibility of an egalitarian definition of ethnic segmentation nor does he, per force, explain why this is not possible. In this respect it seems that Gross, while identifying a real risk, prematurely closes the option for another logical alternative—namely, segmentation without hierarchy. In this manner, the needless contradiction between his two paradigms of ethnicity ensues.

The thrust of Gross's argument is to deny the exclusive use of the organic paradigm based on personal attributes alone, and to complement it with the organizational one in order to enrich the portrait of ethnic community. Though overstating the difference between the two paradigms, he continues with a careful discussion of a methodology for assessment of voluntary associations, using the two criteria of mobilization of resources (members and funds) and goal achievement. At the basis of this analysis is the point that "a mature community is to be found precisely in its ability to sustain purposive organizations" (14). If we accept his analysis, then the challenge to American Jewry lies in the reformulation of its voluntary associations in response to changing circumstances. On the one hand, this reformulation needs to reflect changes in American society, specifically (1) in its normative and political demands, (2) in the needs of its broad-based constituency of Jews, some who do and many who do not affiliate, as well as (3) the relevance and persistence of their continued association. On the other hand, when considering the institutionalization of Israel-Diaspora relations, this needs to reflect ongoing developments, including the changing needs, of Israeli society.

In this context, a new mode of association with Israel will be necessary to sustain the organizational relationship between American Jews and Israel which would be able to enhance American Jewish identity and community. Gross concludes: "The majority of American Jews may increasingly exhibit a tendency to disaffiliate. . . . [T]here is little that one could or should do to prevent individuals from disaffiliating from the community as policy goals are achieved. Successful organizations are those which have been sufficiently flexible to be able to shift domains and redefine intentions" (27).

But to whose intentions is he referring? The role of communal institutions should be properly judged, it may be argued, by the degree that they serve as a platform for a renewed and relevant personal ethnic identity. Institutions which provide a mode of expression for an additional domain or segment of Jewish ethnicity serve to enrich and enhance Jewish life. Israel-centered local institutions could well serve as vehicles for affect and pride as well as a source for collective meaning that may otherwise be lacking in a secularized, symbolically ethnic Jewish world. Jewish philanthropic institutions have long harnessed this power. However it is not at all certain that in their hands alone its effect will be self-sustaining or that its scope can be broadened.

Perhaps a broader communal objective of multistage, multiage bilateral twinning with Israeli communities could be an appropriate response that would redefine Jewish ethnicity in North America. This new formulation would be on the basis of community relations that speak both to commandments and continuity and relate contemporary ethnicity to Jewish peoplehood without being in conflict with the American polity and society.

Such a formulation is the program sponsored by the Jewish Agency and the UJA designed to promote a "living bridge" between Diaspora Jewry and Israel. In this program 27 regions in Israel have been matched with Jewish communities of the Diaspora. Each matched pair maintains a joint lay leadership steering committee to supervise the development and implementation of common objectives in such areas as immigration and absorption, economic development, social networking (people-to-people activities), volunteer programs for both youth and adults, and Israel Experience programs. The premise underlying this new effort is that establishing and strengthening direct Israel-Diaspora relations can enhance Jewish identity and help guarantee Jewish continuity in the Diaspora while serving as a basis for positive social development and change in Israel. At the present time most of this activity occurs primarily among leadership groups. Perhaps only a widespread grassroots-based Israel Experience program will help to disseminate this process down to wider sections of the Jewish community.

THE SYMBOLIC ETHNICITY OF DUAL-IDENTITY HOUSEHOLDS

As both Eisen (1992, 1994) and Waters (1990) have noted, though from quite different perspectives, the ethnic typology of assimilation implies a teleology that is, in fact, neither inevitable nor preferable. It also generates inappropriate strategies that lay at the core of the problematic sociology and optimistic analyses of the American Jewish intelligentsia of the late 1980s.

Sociologists must define the parameters of the symbolic ethnic option, and neither dissolve it into assimilation (rabbinical elites) nor amplify it into generic Judaism (Silberman, 1985). Yet recognizing this option as a sociological one does not determine preference, for it should be seen as a natural outcome of the confluence of modern cultural pluralism, liberalism, and Jewish ethnicity. In terms of our typology, dual-identity households are precisely those that have crossed the rubicon of ethnic constraint. This is so, not necessarily, as Eisen rightly points out, because of an ideological disenchantment with Judaism (or its secularization), but as a structural response to the open Jewish condition of North American Jews (Eisen, 1994:2). Moreover, this is not just an American Jewish option, but rather a universal option for Americans. This option, however, is not available in the same degree for all groups, since as Waters notes, race continues to be an obstacle (Waters, 1990:167-168).

Waters, who also dealt with only one religious group, Roman Catholics, notes that for "white ethnics . . . ethnic identification involves *both* choice and constraint" (Waters, 1990:19). This entails the social construction of ethnic identification on the bases of knowledge of ancestors, family, culture, and such. While this option is most salient for children of mixed marriages, all white

Americans experience this option to differing degrees. Nor does this identification remain constant over time and space. A change in context and biography, then, may call forth different presentations of ethnicity over time.

In the United States, ethnicity is rooted in ancestry, but this becomes confusing when attempting to account for paternal and maternal ties in all ethnic groups, especially in cases of outmarriage. In addition, families with common ancestry are highly unlikely to label children as "American" though mixed families are far more likely to do so (26-33). Waters concludes that "Patterns in the census and survey data, as well as the material from the interviews, show that ethnic identity can change both its importance and its content over the life course and intergenerationally" (51).

THE PERSISTENCE OF SYMBOLIC ETHNICITY IN AMERICA

Why is the route of symbolic ethnicity so easy and attractive to so many Americans, including American Jews? The symbolic ethnicity that Waters refers to is a *soft* option that "does not matter too much." It does not limit choice of marriage partner except across racial boundaries. It does not determine life chances, nor is it prone to negative sanctions. "It matters only in voluntary ways. . . . However in spite of all the ways in which it does not matter, people cling tenaciously to their ethnic identities, they value having an ethnicity and make sure their children know 'where they came from'" (147).

Waters gives the following explanation of this strange persistence that is instructive for students of American Jewish identity. "It stems from two contradictory drives in the American character, a quest for community on the one hand and the desire for individuality on the other. Second, symbolic ethnicity persists because of its ideological "fit" with racist beliefs (147). Waters cites the theorists on American society, from the French visitor Alexis de Tocqueville to Bellah, who stress the tension between individualism and conformity. Modern suburban atomism calls forth a yearning to be from "somewhere," for all urban Americans. Waters goes on to say that "the desire to have a symbolic ethnicity . . . is an attractive and wide spread one despite its lack of demonstrable content because having a symbolic ethnicity combines individuality with feelings both of community . . . that will not interfere with the person's individuality . . . and conformity through an exercise of personal choice" (151).

This community is not a source of commandment, covenant, or commitment; it is uniquely American—that is, neither substance nor absence. Symbolic ethnicity, therefore, is bound to persist for it responds not to biblical or ancestral demands but those of modern life—"a community without cost," a priceless find, a cultural bargain. It is around this dimension of community, rather than ideology, that the future of American Jewish ethnicity may rest.

The negative consequences of symbolic ethnicity for Waters lay in its implications for race relations in America. The very characteristics of flexibility and choice hold inversely for Hispanics and Afro-Americans. The consequences for them are neither symbolic nor voluntary but practical and negative. Waters calls for the universalization of the symbolic option for *all* Americans, so that the celebration of voluntary symbolic ethnicity not become a mechanism for maintaining involuntary ethnic discrimination.

Discrimination and its memory are an ethnic resource. All of Waters's respondents (white, later-generation Catholic descendants of immigrants) cited their ancestors as having been being discriminated against and wanting their children to know about and remember it. "The message of such a belief is that all ethnicities are similar and all will eventually end up successful" (162). This simplistic notion helps explain the resentment to affirmative action policies, for it fails to recognize the structural and historical differences between the options available to white citizens and those that American society offers to its black citizens.

As to the future, a future in which American Jews can expect to fully participate, Waters expects that "Symbolic ethnicity will continue to characterize the ethnicity of later-generation whites . . . yet the . . . dilution of content does not necessarily mean that there will be a decline in the personal satisfaction associated with having a symbolic ethnicity" (166).

The opinion of Jewish elites, whether the so-called federation Jews or the synagogue Jews, concerning the validity, veracity, or viability of contemporary forms of Jewish expression, may have little to do with the reasons why contemporary later-generation Jews continue to affirm their Jewish identity. Still, community leaders need to be able to perceive and respond to new community needs. There may still be time for intervention by community leaders who would like to restructure Jewish community life so that it will be seen by its members as relevant to an emergent American ethnicity.

The literature surveyed here, and its discussion of the American Jewish predicament which it reflects, points to the possible role that Israel and the visit to Israel may play in the newly emerging Jewish ethnicity of modern American Jews. This thesis will be examined more closely and critically in the detailed analysis that follows.

CHAPTER 5

The Israel Connection and the Jewish Question

The elucidation of the connection between Israeli and American Jews requires an analytical understanding of the commonalities and differences between being Jewish in Israel and in North America. This discussion will serve both to sum up and focus our attention on the central topic of this book grounded in the theoretical discussion we have conducted so far. The expressions of contemporary Jewish identity in Israel and North America, sharing the consequences of westernization and modernization, both exhibit macro segmentation of Jewish identity on at least two levels which I will call, respectively, the existential and the theoretical. These two levels are of course not mutually exclusive; they overlap and intersect, representing different levels of abstraction of the same phenomenon. The structure of segmentation at both levels will be presented typologically as two series of continua along each of which Jews can choose to place themselves differentially.

THE EXISTENTIAL MODE

Here five different continua can be distinguished:
1. *Commandment—Choice*: To what extent is Jewish behavior the outcome of a moral obligation or of a cultural option?
2. *Collective—Individualistic*: To what extent are Jewish values the response to a commitment to the collective or the fulfillment of individual desires?
3. *Particular—Universal*: To what extent are Jewish values unique to the Jewish people or merely an expression of values common to all humanity?

4. *Connected—Assimilated*: To what degree does any given Jew feel personally connected or affiliated to the Jewish community or divorced from it, or even belonging to an alternative community?

5. *Distinctive—General*: To what degree is the continuity of the Jewish community itself valued per se, rather than the individual Jew being an invisible part of a larger cultural framework?

At the level of the social world of everyday life, these somewhat abstract dimensions express themselves in the variation and degree of Jewish ritual practice adhered to by modern Jews, the degree to which they are involved in community life, the degree to which they choose to be connected to Jewish institutions and wish their children to do so, the degree to which they interdate and intermarry, and the degree to which they aspire to maintain a separate cultural expression for the Jewishness in their own generation and in that of their grand- children. Each and every one of these questions is shared *both* by Jews in Israel and in the Diaspora, although the content of their substantive responses are shaped by different macro circumstances. In both societies, being Jewish is a matter of choice, but in each context this choice is exercised within a different range, within different contexts, defined by different macro categories of ethnicity and identity.

What, then, are the structural commonalities and differences in the ethnic identity of Jews in Israel and Jews in the Diaspora? Common historical or collective memory and an uncertainty about their future ethnicity are shared by both societies. In each community, secular Jews, especially, are troubled about their ability to transfer this memory to their children and grandchildren, which at the same time leads to a problem of language between the grandchildren in Israel and the grandchildren in the Diaspora. Any resolution of this problem is at least partly dependent on the degree of development of a common language and common experiences.

What, then, is the fundamental structural *difference* between being Jewish in Israel and being Jewish in North America? In one being Jewish is a matter of fact; in the other being Jewish is a matter of choice. In both communities identity is segmented and these segments can be attributed a different weight and a different valence; however, there is a fundamental facticity about being a Jew, no matter how secular, in the sovereign Jewish state that is absent in the existential reality of being a Jew in a non-Jewish Diaspora. In the former, the problem is that being Jewish is taken for granted, while in the latter the problem is that being Jewish *cannot* be taken for granted. In neither case is being Jewish guaranteed by life itself.

THE THEORETICAL MODE

In this mode which recalls the earlier historical discussion on Zionism in America, there are also five distinguishable continua of meaning.

1. *Redemption—Revolution*: This dimension (following Sobel, 1993: 209-210) reflects the fundamental thesis of contemporary Zionism which asserted that, instead of waiting for divine redemption, Jewish salvation could be achieved by human collective intervention or decisive action. The revolution called for the establishment of a sovereign Jewish state with a new Jewish identity characterized by certain transformations. The first transformation is an activist relationship to redemption; the second, a secular option for secular identity *either in place of the religious or alongside of it*; third, the renaissance of the Hebrew language.

2. *Religious—Secular*: This continuum relates to the degree to which religion is the defining characteristic of Jewish identity. In Israel it is important to note the profound ethnic difference between Ashkenazi and Sephardi Jews on this issue. The Zionism of Ashkenazi Jews can be characterized as revolutionary, for it sought to change the Jews themselves as well as their objective situation (living in minority status in the Diaspora); the Zionism of the Sephardi Jews, however, was essentially redemptive, for it sought essentially to change only the Jews' objective situation to return them to Zion, in order to fulfill them though not to change them. The State of Israel remains, then, with the competing ideologies of the secular Zionism of its Ashkenazi founders and the religious traditionalism of its Sephardi citizenry.

3. *People—Nation*: While the biblical historical primacy of peoplehood to nationality is well known, in contemporary Israel second- and third-generation Israelis may well rank being Israeli *before* being Jewish; in America, moreover, Jews of the same generation may well rank being American *before* being Jewish as well as granting a lesser or greater role to the place of Israel in their personal identity.

4. *Israel—Diaspora*: Contemporary Zionism has negated the Diaspora, both ideologically and existentially. It has negated the legitimacy and the efficacy of minority existence in a non-Jewish world and demanded exclusivity as the solution to the problems of the Jewish people. After World War II the Diaspora in turn rejected this negation and with it the moral imperative for migration to Israel (aliya), and has instead sanctified philanthropy as a legitimate expression of support for Israel. This support draws on widespread pro-Israel sentiment and provides the Jewish institutional elites with an avenue of participation in contemporary Jewish nation building without being personally in the national homeland. Third- and fourth- generation Jews in Israel and in the Diaspora share, for the most part, a reciprocal negation of each others' exclusive claims to legitimacy with a concomitant reciprocal ignorance of the others' distinctive Jewish culture either as an object or as a possible resource.

5. *Normative Community—Affective Community*: The aggregate outcome of the differential appropriation of dimensions of individual identity and the different levels of theoretical identity may be either communities that are based to a high degree on shared values and precepts or communities that

are primarily based on kinship and affect. Communities can, of course, be characterized by both: the degree to which they are may be a sign of ethnic strength, just as the degree to which an individual has access neither to a community of affect nor to a community of values would indicate his or her situation of isolation and probably assimilation.

If the existential mode of segmentation provides the recipe knowledge of how to "do Jewish," the theoretical mode provides the language of legitimacy and authority in contemporary Jewish life. Segmentation on this mode, by definition, questions any unidimensional or exclusive bases of Jewish legitimacy. Thus, the claims for legitimacy are contested and struggled over by competing elites, leaving the rank and file on their own to resolve in their everyday life. Contests of Jewish legitimacy, however, are not identical in Israel and North America. The question of whether to be religious or not is culturally different in Israel from North America; the question of legitimacy of denominational pluralism, as well, is perceived differently in North America than it is in Israel.

The Israel connection itself, if there is to be one, stands at the interface between these contrasting and contested bases of legitimacy. Yet the very prosaic fact of Israel's growth, size, and permanence will undoubtedly be a source for restructuring the different ideologies of Jewish life, both in Israel and North America, sharing common roots in nineteenth century Europe. Similarly, the enduring existence of strong Diaspora Jewish communities will require a rapprochement between the Zionism of the majority of Israelis and their elites and the widespread pro-Israel sentiment of the majority of North American Jews and their elites if Jewish peoplehood is to be sustained.

UNIFIED IDENTITY—SEGMENTED IDENTITY

Both of these former modes of segmentation of identity allow us now to look at contemporary Jewish identity on two overarching dimensions. The first dimension is the degree to which identity is a unified, as compared to segmented, identity. In contemporary Israel, for example, the attempts of radical religious Zionists to over identify religious law (*Halacha*) with the *polis* (state) would be only one extreme expression of a unified identity which cannot be shared by many segments of the population. Thus, in Israel too, under the umbrella of the sovereign state, Jews have no alternative but to choose different segments and different rankings of importance of these segments as well as different levels of unity between them.

The second dimension is the degree to which identity is ethnic or symbolic. In North America this same option of choice expresses itself in the typology between ethnic identity and symbolic identity which has been amply discussed above.

Throughout this discussion, Jewish identity has not been presented from a normative perspective, whether rabbinic or secular, nor has it been dependent on a normative judgment. The analysis is not contingent on an affirmation of a particular ideology, either the religious or the secular, the Zionist or the non-Zionist, or of one denomination rather than another. It recognizes that there are a plurality of dimensions which make up contemporary Jewish culture world-wide and different modalities of expression and identification within that culture, including the question of whether one ought to be identified with it at all. The connection between different Jews in North America and different Jews in the State of Israel, between Jewish communities in North America and communities of Jews in Israel, may then be a reflection of what they choose to be their common ground on each of the continua outlined above. It will be suggested in what follows that the Israel visit may be an important element within the multidimensional contemporary North American Jewish identity, both as a symbol to identify with and as an experience to be lived through. To the extent that Jewish experiences and settings are common to Jews in Israel and in the Diaspora, so may the commonalities of their contemporary Jewish identity be generated and shared.

CHAPTER 6

Methodology

THE SAMPLE POPULATION

The sampling procedure used for NJPS has been discussed extensively in the literature (Kosmin et al., 1991:30-39; Goldstein and Goldstein, 1996:24-29), and in the Waksberg methodological appendix of the latter volume. Three stages of data collection were implemented. Stage I involved a national sample drawn through random digit dialing (RDD) of the total U.S. population representing all religions as well as the secular. Random digit dialing gives all households with telephones in the United States (both Jewish and non-Jewish) a known chance of selection into the sample so that federation or other lists are not necessary. Stage I consisted of four screening questions asked over the course of the year of the 125,813 randomly selected households, in the following order:

1. What is your religion? If not Jewish, then . . . .
2. Do you or anyone else in the household consider themselves Jewish? If no, then . . . .
3. Were you or anyone else in the household raised Jewish? If no, then . . . .
4. Do you or anyone else in the household have a Jewish parent?

   Stage I yielded 5,146 households which contained at least one person who qualified as Jewish or Jewishly affiliated by the screening questions.

   During Stage II, potential respondents were recontacted, and Jewish households who met the survey qualifications moved on to the final interviewing phase, Stage III, which yielded a total of 2,441 in-depth interviews with Jewish respondents aged 18 and over who constitute a representative national sample of Jewish households. Persons qualified to be respondents in the survey if they indicated they were Jewish by religion, considered themselves Jewish, or were born/raised Jewish. Households were included in the sample only if they contained at least one qualified respondent. The analysis in this present study is not based on the total NJPS sample referred to as the "extended" Jewish population, but is restricted to respondents representing the "core" Jewish population, N=2,061. This core population represents some 5.5 million American Jews, including (1) those who were born Jewish and reported their current religion as Jewish, (2) those who identified themselves as Jewish when asked but reported no current religion, and (3) persons who are currently Jewish but were born Gentile. The core sample does not include those who were born or raised Jewish but switched out, or those who have Jewish parents but were raised in another religion. The total number of respondents excluded from the total NJPS sample for the purpose of the present study is 380, representing 16 percent of the total sample.

The national perspective of the NJPS data is no doubt its most important strength. This perspective makes it possible to assess the relative impact of an Israel visit on the various segments of North American Jewry controlling for both the nature of their Jewish identity and other variables. Nonetheless, it is important to bear in mind some of the data's weaknesses. First, the size of the sample often creates difficulties for multilevel analyses. This problem was especially acute with the numerous questions dealing with issues of Jewish identity and continuity that were restricted to a module subsample of only one-third the total sample. Questions so restricted include Jewish parentage of respondent, the age at which visit(s) to Israel occurred, and other variables related to Israel. Second, because of the omnibus character of the survey, important additional questions related to Israel visits were not asked at all, such as the purpose of the visit, and whether or not the respondent was satisfied with the logistic, educational, and experiential components of the visit, and its later impact on attitudinal and behavioral factors.

To compensate for some of these, chapter 12 of this book uses additional data for supplemental and comparative purposes. Some of these data, as noted earlier, are taken from the 1991 New York Jewish Population Study as well as the Boston CJP Demographic Study (Israel, 1998). Both studies resemble the NJPS in the use of a cross-sectional methodology and in content. The New York survey allows for a more accurate analysis of the subsection of youth as a result of a much larger sampling size (N=4,006), while the Boston study is important as the most recent study in the domain because it includes new questions on the age of the first visit to Israel of respondents. For the sake of simplicity, the comparison between NJPS and NYJPS will be made only between Jews by religion from both data sets, primarily because of the small population of secular Jews in New York. The sampling procedure and methodology for the NYJPS can be found in Horowitz (1993). In chapter 12 we will also compare longitudinal data of one Israel Experience program, Project Otzma. This monitoring and evaluation study has been conducted by the author on a regular basis since the inception of the program in 1986.

THE VARIABLES

Three sets of variables are derived using the data gathered in the 1990 National Jewish Population Survey. The first set measures the frequency of visiting Israel, as well as the duration and timing of the last visit. Of the 623 respondents who have visited Israel we have the timing of their last visit for only 35 percent (N=216). Of these 216 respondents of all ages who have ever visited Israel, only 50 percent have visited since 1980. Therefore, these data related to the timing of the visit are inadequate for statistical analysis.

The second set of measures consists of demographic and socioeconomic background information about the sample respondents. These measures enable us to discriminate between those who have been to Israel and those who have not through the presentation of the demographic, denominational, and socioeconomic profiles of (1) those who have never visited Israel, (2) those who have visited only once, and (3) those who did so more often. On the basis of descriptive data we examine the differences, if any, between the three groups on these background dimensions, as well as on simple and compound measures of Jewish religious practice and Jewish community affiliation. The objective is to identify factors affecting visits to Israel such as socioeconomic status and life-cycle concerns. The third level of analysis is an investigation of the relationship between the Israel visit and the three measures of Jewish identification (Jewish religious practice, communal affiliation, and outmarriage), holding constant background factors such as age, gender, family, region, income, Jewish schooling, and denomination.

Thus, the visit to Israel will be treated in two different ways, first as a dependent variable and later as an independent variable. The first allows explanation of the characteristics of the people who visit Israel and at what rate people visit Israel. By work experience Tables 14 through 29, among others, for example, illustrate that the visit to Israel is an outcome variable, while such factors as age, gender, Jewish education, and denomination are the explanatory or independent variables. The hypothesis here, then, is that the more Jewish education a respondent has, the more likely he or she is to visit Israel.

In the second mode, the visit to Israel, sometimes separately and sometimes together with another factor such as Jewish education, is treated as an independent variable—that is, the explaining variable. In that analysis we attempt to examine the degree to which the visit to Israel is associated differentially with measures of Jewish behavior and identification—for example, the degree to which having visited Israel on one or more occasions is likely to be associated with an increase in the score of Jewish religious practice, Jewish communal affiliation, and rates of outmarriage.

THE PROBLEM OF CAUSAL INFERENCE IN NJPS

This question of the role of the Israel visit is critical and highlights the inherent limitations of attempting to infer cause and effect from any study that is based on cross-sectional data in general and the NJPS data in particular. A cross-sectional survey can still collect retrospective, longitudinal life history data, while NJPS was not able to do so because of the omnibus character of the survey and the limited time available for in-depth attention to particular topics. Therefore, what is in principle possible with cross-sectional data is to control for background variables which are regarded as correlates for previsit levels of measures of Jewish identification such as Jewish religious practice and Jewish affiliation at least of the parental home. This allows a rough approximation of pre- and post-analysis where the visit to Israel is considered to be the independent variable.

To achieve this goal, the convention applied by social science is, in this case, to examine the relationship between a visit to Israel and measures of Jewish practice while controlling successively for the variables that might render themselves the "real" explanation for the outcome of the data. "Controlling" refers to the practice whereby the relationship between two variables such as the visit to Israel and religious practice is examined, while comparing groups that share a third characteristic, such as Jewish education, thus isolating the presumed effect of the latter. This is the strategy adopted herein. Our objective is to assess, with appropriate caution, what may be learned about the correlation of a visit to Israel, relative to other variables, to measurements of Jewish identity.

The analysis will utilize two methods of statistical analysis: bivariate and multivariate. In bivariate analysis, we examine single correlations between two variables, such as the visit to Israel and the Index of Jewish Religious Practice, each time controlling for a single third variable, such as Jewish education. This analysis is done for many such pairs, though only one at a time.

The second approach will be conducted through multiple classification analysis. In this analysis the visit to Israel "competes" with respondents' other background variables that are correlates of previsit Jewish practice in explaining measures of respondents' Jewish practice in 1990. This method takes us one step further by the simultaneous analysis of a number of explanatory independent variables with a single dependent variable. This is accomplished by controlling first for each of the independent variables separately and then all of them cumulatively. The statistical assumption here is that if the visit to Israel is a mere correlate, reflection, or outcome of any one of the other *competing* independent explanatory variables such as Jewish education or denomination, in the explanation of variance in Jewish religious practice, then the weight of the Israel visit will be statistically insignificant. If, however, such an analysis shows that after taking account of the other independent variables which are included in the model, the visit to Israel continues to contribute to a statistically significant degree to the explanation of variance in the dependent variable, then it can be argued, within the limits of parametric analysis of cross-sectional data, that the hypothesis of its presumed independent association has been supported.

Multiple classification analysis goes beyond the previous bivariate analysis since in addition to determining the weight of the Israel visit in its own right, it also estimates the weight of the visit to Israel while controlling for all other independent variables in the model. By this procedure it is possible to test the hypothesis that, *regardless of the background the respondent has come from,* an Israel visit makes it more likely that he or she will have a higher score on measures of Jewish identity such as Jewish religious practice or Jewish communal affiliation.

In addition to the analysis of the NJPS data, comparative cross-validation has been attained by the selective use of the New York Jewish Population data set. Methodologically critical to this study is the inclusion of the longitudinal data set of the follow-up study of the one-year Otzma program. In this case, measures of Jewish identity are available for respondents at the beginning of the visit to Israel, at its conclusion, and even on their return to North America. The data, moreover, include information concerning home background, Jewish schooling, and previous visits to Israel. Consequently, the data present no difficulty in establishing time sequence or in controlling for background variables. Thus, inferences for causality with respect to the impact of the Israel visit can be more powerfully sustained.

CHAPTER 7

The Core Jewish Population
of North America

The distribution of "core" Jewish respondents in this study is as follows: (a) Jewish by religion, 77 percent (respondents who were born Jewish and reported current religion as Jewish); (b) born Jewish, 19 percent (respondents who were born Jewish but identify with no religion); and (c) Jewish by choice, 4 percent (respondents born Gentile but chose to be Jewish) (Table 3). As noted earlier, excluded from this study are respondents of Jewish descent who reported a religion other than Judaism.

AGE, GENERATION, AND GENDER

The core Jewish population is spread over four or more generations of Jews living in the United States, beginning with the immigrant and second generation who have resided the longest time in America, followed by the third, fourth, and fifth generations. This analysis examines three age groups; 18-34, 35-44, and 45 and over. The plurality, 44 percent, of the adult core Jewish respondents are in the 45 and over age group, while 33 percent are in the 18-34 age group, and 24 percent are in the 35-44 age group. The third-generation constitutes 40 percent of the total core Jewish population, and 52 percent of all 35-44 year olds are third generation core Jews. Moreover, 37 percent of this age group belong to the fourth generation. The fourth generation makes up 31 percent of the total core Jewish population. Fifty-four percent of 18-34 year old core Jews are fourth-generation Jews compared to only 10 percent of those 45 years and over (Table 4). Division by gender among the core Jewish respondents reflects the larger population with 48 percent male respondents and 52 percent female respondents. This imbalance is greatest among the 18 to 34 year olds (Table 5). (This may be due, in part, to the cumulative self-selective effect of immigration and mortality in earlier generations. It may also be attributable to the gender bias of outmarriage of previous generations favoring men, a trend which is currently being reversed with the more even distribution of outmarriage between Jewish men and women.) Of the core Jewish population of adults over 18, 63 percent are married, 22 percent were never married, and 15 percent were divorced, separated, or widowed.

JEWISH IDENTIFICATION, GENERATION, AND DENOMINATION

The historical transformation of American Jewish ethnicity from one of an immigrant group with shared values to a voluntary community with shared feelings points to the dynamic and even volatile nature of the structure and content of American Jewish ethnicity. Is it possible to pinpoint the sociological parameters of that change? When looking at Jewish identification over generations, we notice that the *fourth generation has the fewest number of respondents who identify as Jewish by religion (59 percent).* Among *earlier* generations we find that between *82 percent and 90 percent of the respondents identify as Jewish by religion.* Thirty-one percent of the respondents belonging to the fourth generation identify themselves as ethnic and secular, while 10 percent are Jewish by choice. The other three generations include only a small number of Jews by choice, 1-2 percent. The fourth generation has the maximum proportion (31 percent) who identify as ethnic and secular as compared to 15 percent in the first generation (Table 3).

The denominational structure of American Jewry has changed over the generations. The NJPS makes it possible to distinguish between the present denomination of the adult respondents and the denomination in which they were raised. Significant differences are found between the two types of denominational classifications and the respective changes over generations. Beginning with denomination raised, we can see in Table 6a that 69 percent of American Jews are currently of the third and fourth generations. Examining their response to "denomination raised," 46 percent of third-generation respondents were raised as Conservative, 33 percent were raised as Reform, and 16 percent were raised as Orthodox. While the percentage of Jews who were raised as Conservative drops from 46 percent in the third generation to 35 percent in the fourth generation, the percentage of Reform rises from 33 percent in the third generation to 50 percent in the fourth generation. This testifies to a dramatic historical increase in the number of Reform Jews.

At the same time, if we look at "current denomination," the number of fourth-generation Jews who are currently Conservative is only 23 percent and the number of currently Reform is 40 percent. Among fourth-generation respondents, the number of nondenominational, or other, respondents rises to 34 percent from 24 percent in the third generation (Table 6b). It appears, then, that young American Jews are moving away from Orthodoxy and Conservative Judaism toward Reform Judaism, while Reform Jews are leaving the denominational fold altogether. It is these current Reform and "other" Jews who are prime candidates for contemporary symbolic ethnicity. Looking at the population in this way shows that as the third and fourth generations less frequently identify with the Jewish community through religion, they identify more as secular, or Jews with no religion. But who are these ethnic secular Jews?

The answer is that only half of all ethnic secular respondents have two Jewish parents (54 percent), compared to 87 percent of respondents who are Jewish by religion and 76 percent of all core Jews. The Jewish parent in the majority of cases of ethnic Jews is the father (Tables 7a and 7b). Not surprisingly, then, there is a strong positive correlation between having parents who had married out and outmarriage of the respondent. In fact, these respondents have the highest rate of out marriage among the current Jewish population

Analysis of the module subsample reconfirms the relationship between first- and second-generation outmarriage. As we can see from Table 7b, among all core Jewish respondents both of whose parents are Jewish, 32 percent of those married are currently married to a Gentile spouse. Among those respondents with only a Jewish father, 88 percent of those married are married to a Gentile spouse. Similarly, among those core Jewish respondents with only a Jewish mother, 78 percent of those married are currently married to a Gentile spouse. Ethnic secular Jews, therefore, are generally people with parents who are outmarried and/or who are outmarried themselves. They reflect the cumulative effect of outmarriage over generations and constitute *31 percent of all current fourth generation core Jews.*

Among respondents who identify as Jewish by religion, 27 percent of respondents with two Jewish parents are currently married to a Gentile spouse. In addition, 88 percent of Jews by religion with only a Jewish father are married to a Gentile spouse, while 72 percent with a Jewish mother only are married to a Gentile spouse. Ethnic secular respondents show the highest rate of outmarriage with 69 percent of respondents with two Jewish parents currently married to a Gentile spouse. Ninety-three percent of ethnic secular respondents with only a Jewish father are married to a Gentile spouse and 100 percent of ethnic secular respondents with only a Jewish mother are married to a Gentile spouse (Table 7c).

The denominations the core Jewish respondents currently identify with are Orthodox (5 percent), Conservative (32 percent), Reform (37 percent), and "other" (9 percent), including Reconstructionist (1.2 percent), and "just Jewish" (7.8 percent). Seventeen percent identify with no denomination at all (Table 8). It may be that this denominational pattern, which is somewhat different from those reported in other national studies (though closer to the findings of various local demographic studies), reflects the more inclusive methodology and criteria used in developing the NJPS 1990 survey sample discussed above. This difference is reflected in the survey's inclusion of households where two consecutive generations have outmarried, meaning one of the parents and at least one of the grandparents are Gentile. While the inclusion of second-generation outmarrieds is not desirable, it does need to be noted and controlled for when examining the association between any two variables. Thus if Cohen and Rosen's 1992 study of Jewish affiliation shows a denominational distribution consisting of 10 percent Orthodox, 34 percent Conservative, 33 percent Reform, this is because 99 percent of their sample was "either born Jewish or converted", (7) though even in their study only 72 percent were married to Jewish spouses.

REGION

Studies on regional differences provide valuable information for the recruitment for Israel experience programs. A recent report (Cohen, 1995a) has shown significant regional differences in teen-age rates of participation in short-term Israel programs. Cohen identifies three Israel program participation indicators which help to explain varying rates of participation: (1) population size, (2) income levels, and (3) synagogue affiliation (217). Clearly, it is the smaller, wealthier, and more affiliated communities which send the largest contingents of young Jews to Israel.

In addition, the 1970/71 NJPS reported a high rate of mobility among American Jewry, resulting in the changing distribution of the Jewish population in regions throughout the country. This geographic mobility in turn led to the growth or decline of many local Jewish communities by "reducing the opportunities for integration locally and by increasing opportunities for greater interaction with non-Jews . . ." (Goldstein, 1993:95). On the other hand, the dispersion of Jews throughout the country may also have a positive effect, as Goldstein notes, by adding to the population of dwindling Jewish communities and perhaps providing the help needed to build and maintain facilities and institutions essential for Jewish community.

The Northeastern United States is home to 43 percent of the U.S. core Jewish respondents. This is the highest concentration of core Jewish respondents found in one region. In contrast, the Midwest is home to the lowest percentage of Jewish respondents, only 11 percent. The Southern and Western regions of the United States have equal populations of core Jewish respondents, 23 percent (Table 9). The region with the youngest population is the Midwest, with 35 percent of the 18-34 age group. The Southern region has both a high concentration of younger and older respondents, 34 percent and 45 percent, respectively. The demographic dynamics that underlie these data have been discussed by Kosmin et al. (1991).

EDUCATIONAL ATTAINMENT: JEWISH AND GENERAL

Respondents were asked, "What was the major type of schooling you received for your formal Jewish education?" and "How many years of formal

Jewish education did you receive?" These two questions constitute the basis for the triple classification of Jewish educational attainment. (Medding et al., 1992) The three groups are: (1) those respondents (34 percent) who received no Jewish education at all; (2) those (43 percent) who received a low level of Jewish education—namely, less than six years of afternoon school or Sunday school; and (3) those (23 percent) who received more than six years of afternoon school or any amount of day school (Table 10). Ten percent of all core Jewish respondents indicate that day school was their major form of Jewish education, 77 percent of whom attended day school for six years or more. An additional 14 percent attended day school for four or five years. Thus, only 9 percent actually attended day school for a small number of years. Day school alumni who attended for five years or less received virtually the same scores on indices of Jewish identity and behavior, including outmarriage, as did alumni of afternoon school of more than six years.

This distribution of Jewish educational attainment stands in stark contrast to scores received on general educational attainment, where 64 percent of core Jewish respondents possessed a college degree or had engaged in postgraduate work (Table 11). While the two forms of educational attainment (Jewish and general) are correlated (i.e. overlap), it is still the case that among respondents with a college degree, 47 percent report having received a weak Jewish education and an additional 30 percent reported having received no Jewish education at all.

INCOME AND JEWISH EDUCATION

Questions concerning household income are problematic for several reasons. A significant number of respondents, 13 percent, chose not to answer the income question in the NJPS survey. The nonresponse rate was even higher, 19 percent, in the New York survey. Furthermore, household income here is utilized as a broad indicator of socioeconomic status of the individual respondent. It is not a measure of the actual income earned by the respondent except for single-person households. The median range income of the national subsample is $40,000-$49,000, whereas the mode is $30,000-$39,000. These income figures are somewhat lower than those in the New York study, where the median household income was reported to be $50,000. The disparity is due primarily to a higher number of single-person households in the NJPS. In this study, we have divided household income into the three categories: (1) $39,000 or less, (2) $40,000-$79,999, and (3) $80,000 or more.

Forty-four percent of the core Jewish respondents are concentrated in the combined household income bracket of $39,999 or less; 37 percent are in the middle-income bracket of $40,000-$79,999, while only 19 percent are in the high-income-earning bracket of $80,000 or more (Table 12). The findings indicate that the cutoff point where income made a difference in the dependent variable of Israel visits was at the $80,000 income level and higher.

Is the degree of Jewish education of the respondents related to current levels of household income? Since the data presented below compare current (adult) income of the respondents with their Jewish schooling as children, no direct relationship between them may be inferred. Our intention here is not to imply that Jewish education affects income in later life. The purpose of explaining family socioeconomic status is to investigate the ability of families to send their children to Jewish schools. Thus it is instructive to observe the pattern that emerges between Jewish educational attainment and socioeconomic status of adult alumni.

The lower income category, $39,999 or less, has the highest rate, 39 percent, of respondents with no Jewish education, while among the highest income bracket only 20 percent had no Jewish education. The relationship between income and Jewish education holds true in each age group but especially among those in the lower income category aged 18-34, where 45 percent reported having no Jewish education. Thus if the respondent is in the 18-34 age category, residing in a household with an income of $39,000 or less, the chances are higher that they will have had no Jewish education at all. The highest income bracket of the same age indicates only 21 percent with no Jewish education. This same trend, which associates higher income with higher Jewish education, is reflected in all age groups. The lower income 18-34 year old age group, when compared to any other age group and income bracket, has the most members, 45 percent, with no Jewish education (Table 13). It is clear that Jewish education is distributed differentially among different income groups. The higher income group had more Jewish education than the lower income group. As shall be seen, this finding suggests consequences for Jewish continuity, which, perhaps, has priced itself out of the market.

CHAPTER 8

Visits to Israel

THE VISIT TO ISRAEL AND JEWISH IDENTIFICATION

The overall rate of visiting Israel is not particularly high. Thirty-one percent of all respondents who are Jewish by religion have visited Israel at least once, while only 11 percent of either secular Jews or Jews by choice have visited Israel (Figure 3). We conclude therefore that people who identify with being Jewish by religion are more likely to visit Israel than respondents who do not identify with the Jewish religion.

Figure 3
Visit to Israel: Core Jews

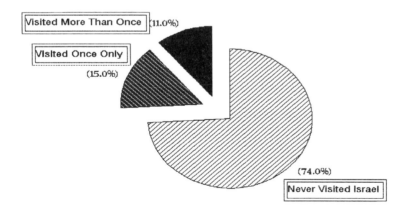

THE VISIT TO ISRAEL: HOW OFTEN AND FOR HOW LONG

Overall, as we have seen above, 26 percent of all core Jews have visited Israel (Table 14). Among those who have visited, 59 percent remained for as long as three weeks (Figure 4). Age is clearly related to the length of stay. Forty-three percent of respondents under the age of 45 were more likely to have visited Israel for over two months compared to only 8 percent of respondents age 45 and over (Table 15). This indicates that a longer stay in Israel is more characteristic of today's younger generation than that of its parents or grandparents, and that a longer stay is probably more likely to be undertaken at a younger rather than older age.

Figure 4
Duration of Longest Visit to Israel of All Core Jews

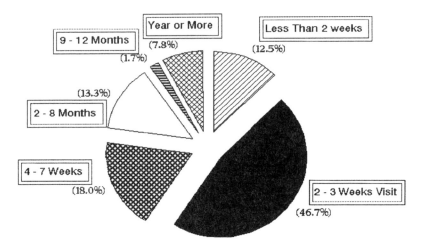

A longer visit tends to be more frequent among those who have visited Israel on more than one occasion (Table 16). In this category, 52 percent have visited Israel for longer than three weeks, about half have visited up to seven weeks, with the remainder having visited up to one year. A stay for a period of over two months is a fairly strong indicator of someone who has been to Israel more than once. By contrast only 13 percent of first-time visitors stayed for a longer period.

In addition, the duration of an Israel visit is also associated with the marital status and age of a respondent. We can see from examining Table 17 that respondents who are not married stay in Israel longer. Forty-four percent of respondents who are not married have visited Israel once for a period of one to eight months, while a much smaller number of married respondents, 24 percent, visited Israel once for the same period of time. When making a further distinction between those who have visited Israel once and those who have visited more than once, analyzed by age, we find that among the 18-34 year olds the percentage of first-time visitors who remain in Israel for a period of two months or longer reaches 55 percent compared to 50 percent of 35-44 year olds and 13 percent of respondents 45 and over. These results are an outcome of the effect of age and the cohort. By the same token, the data from the 1990 survey show us that 67 percent of once-only visitors to Israel *over* the age of 45 visited for only three weeks or less (Table 18).

THE VISIT TO ISRAEL BY GENDER AND AGE

Men and women visit Israel with approximately the same overall frequency. Of those who have visited Israel only once, 54 percent are women and 46 percent are men (Table 19). On the other hand, of those who visit more than once, more are men (53%) than are women (Figure 5).

Figure 5
Visits to Israel by Gender

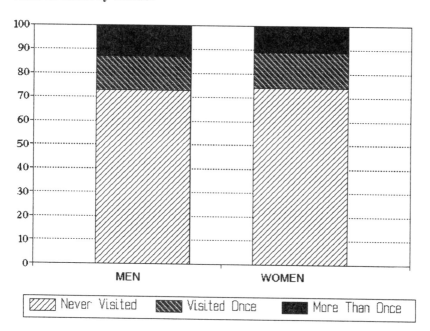

People 45 years old and older visit Israel more often than others. Seventeen percent of 45-64 year olds have visited Israel once compared to 20 percent of those 65 and over. It should be noted that while 15 percent of all core Jews have visited Israel once, 26 percent of this group are 65 or older. While 11 percent of 45-64 year olds have visited Israel more than once, 21 percent of those who have visited more than once are aged 65 and over.

In the two youngest age groups, the rate of visiting Israel one time was 12 percent (Table 20). In the 18-34 age bracket, 10 percent have visited more than once and 8 percent of 35-44 year olds have visited more than once (Figure 6).

Figure 6
Visits to Israel by Age

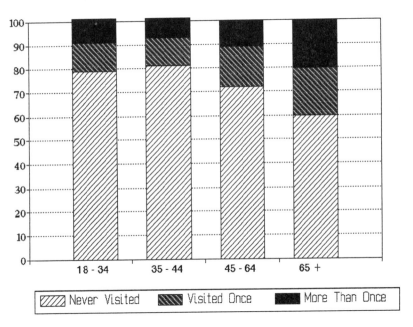

Twenty-eight percent of married respondents have visited Israel (15 percent once and 13 percent more than once), as have 22 percent of the never-marrieds (13 percent once and 9 percent more than once). However, in the age category 18-34, 24 percent of the singles have visited Israel in contrast to only 18 percent of the marrieds. Of interest here is that trips to Israel tend to occur more among those under 35 and those over 50 with a hiatus in between. The ability to visit Israel is contingent upon such factors as time, money, and inclination, and the members of these two age groups are more likely to possess these characteristics. The lower rate among young married couples is due in large part to the focus on building a home, raising children, and establishing a career.

Jewish leaders wishing to address the issue of the potential impact of a visit to Israel on the life choices of participants should recognize that their primary target group is under 35 years old.

THE VISIT TO ISRAEL BY REGION

There are only slight differences among the regions of the United States with regard to the rate of visiting Israel. The somewhat notable exception is the South with a high rating of 31 percent. The lowest is the West with 23 percent, with the Northeast and Midwest scoring 26 percent and 24 percent, respectively (Figure 7).

Figure 7
Visits to Israel by Age and Region

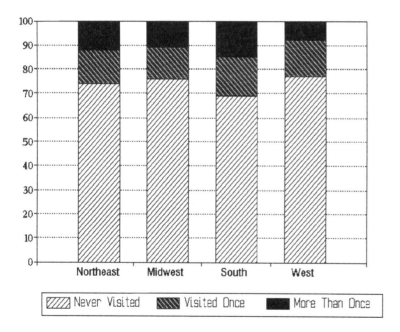

When comparison between regions is made while controlling for age, it is important to note the regional differences in age composition. The transplanting of Jews from the Northeast to the South results in a smaller than expected number of visitors from the Northeast and a larger than expected number from the South. Thus, it is perhaps not surprising to discover that older persons from the southern part of the United States are more frequent visitors than older persons from the rest of the country. The average age of visitors from the South is skewed by retirees from Florida. In the South, 44 percent of persons over the age of 45 are visitors, compared to 30-33 percent in other regions (Table 21). When the regions are compared while controlling for age we find that in the 18-34 age category, the Northeast and Midwest have a significantly higher rate of visitors to Israel, 24 percent and 25 percent respectively, than do the South, 18 percent, and the West, 16 percent.

The Midwest reflects the migration out of the area by retirees and seniors, which leads to the unusual situation of a declining population in which the average age decreases over time. This contrasts to most situations of migration and population decline, in which it is the younger people who move, leaving a community which becomes increasingly older.

THE VISIT TO ISRAEL BY INCOME AND AGE

Household income levels do not seem to make a significant difference in the rate of visiting Israel when comparing low and moderate income earning groups. Respondents reporting lower income have visited Israel once at the same rate as moderate income respondents (14 percent). However, the high-income-earning group, $80,000 and more, has visited Israel far more frequently than both other income groups. Eighteen percent of the respondents in this group have visited Israel once, while 13 percent have visited more than once. In other words, the high-income-earning group represents 31 percent of those who ever visited, compared to 23 percent in the two other income categories (Table 22). Although the response to current income may not reflect the respondents' economic level at the time of their visits, income level is a general indicator of socioeconomic status of the respondents.

Household income is a poor differentiator between those who visit Israel and those who do not. This is probably because, as we have already seen from the data, a trip to Israel comes generally later in life when the respondents have long passed their critical economic thresholds and have more discretionary income available. The economics of travel and tourism are not just a function of household income or even personal discretionary income, but, as Bull (1991) has pointed out, there is an entire set of macro- and microeconomic forces which influence the likelihood of a tourist visit and its character, destination, and duration. The tourist is often required to sacrifice scarce resources, including money and time, each of which has an "opportunity cost" attached.

Bull presents a formal Lancasterian economic model which analyzes tourism as an outcome of the relationship between disposable income, available free time, prices of travel components, and the time necessary to implement each component. This analysis allows us to understand why a tourist with a declining income but fixed vacation time may simply choose a cheaper holiday of equal length, while wealthy tourists who are short on time may buy an expensive but short travel package. In this model, the decision to travel is affected by the differential costs of travel components. International airfares vary considerably from state to state. The domestic portion of a flight to Israel from Tucson or

Ontario, for instance, is almost $500, while for Chicago, Miami, or St. Louis the domestic portion of a flight to Israel is less than half that amount.

Bull, utilizing a typology of travel and tourism similar to my own earlier work (Mittelberg, 1988:29-35), discriminates between visiting friends and relatives (VFR) and vacation, where the latter is more income elastic than the former. In these terms, visiting friends and relatives in Israel should be less prone to drops in income than an ordinary holiday or vacation, while convention and business tourism is less sensitive to income changes than both of the former (Bull, 1991:38).

Bull utilizes the notion of "opportunity cost" or "the lost opportunity of using it in the (presumably next best activity)" (159). This measure of economic resources is applied by potential tourists, both to their time and their money. For example, young adults can be perceived to attribute a low opportunity cost to the time at their disposal, yet a high premium on their disposable income. While lower prices may not affect economically established tourists, they could make a significant difference to young adults. The latter would then visit once and, having done so, visit for a longer period of time than the older and wealthier.

Thirty-one percent of the core Jewish respondents in the high-income category have visited Israel at least once in comparison to 24 percent of the low- income category. This pattern is consistent for each age group, indicating that people with a high income visit Israel more frequently. This is especially true in the 45 and over age group, where only 30 percent of the low-income group has visited Israel compared to 39 percent of the high income group (Table 23). What this implies is that a subsidy for first-time, young adult, single visitors could have a leverage effect on the rate of visiting Israel, a finding that supports earlier conclusions by Steven Cohen (1986).

THE VISIT TO ISRAEL BY JEWISH AND GENERAL EDUCATIONAL ATTAINMENT

Core Jews who reported a high level of Jewish education have the highest rate of visiting Israel (47 percent), compared to those who reported a low level of Jewish education (23 percent) and those who reported having received no Jewish education (17 percent), (Figure 8). Clearly, the higher one's level of Jewish education the more likely one is to visit Israel. However, the tie between Jewish education and visiting Israel is multifaceted. On one hand, the more intensive the degree of Jewish education the more likely one is to visit Israel. However, it must also be taken into account that the likelihood of visiting Israel also reflects the economic power of the Jewish household and its "roll on" effect in the role that the usually expensive private Jewish high schools play in encouraging and often subsidizing Israel visits.

Figure 8
Visits to Israel by Jewish Education

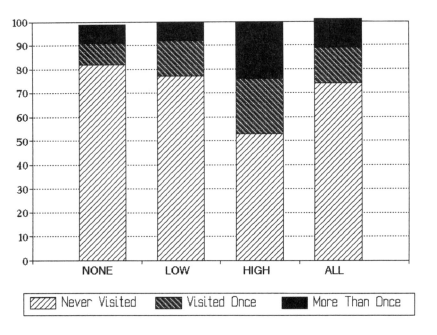

Respondents with a high level of general education—that is, who have formally studied beyond a bachelor's degree—display a higher rate of visiting Israel (35 percent) than people with only a bachelor's degree (24 percent). In every age category respondents with a college education visited Israel to a greater degree than respondents with only a high school education (Table 25).

THE VISIT TO ISRAEL BY DENOMINATION AND JEWISH PARENTAGE

The relationship between denomination and visiting Israel follows a hierarchical pattern in relation to religious ideology; 60 percent of Orthodox, 39 percent of Conservative, 23 percent of Reform, and 21 percent of other core Jews have ever visited Israel (Figure 9). The greater tendency of traditionally observant Jews to visit Israel has been well established (Cohen, 1986, Hochstein, 1986). This is in line with the earlier analysis which shows the undifferentiated and universally low representation often given to the numbers who visit Israel from the United States. At the same time, it points to the potential negative implications regarding connections to Israel for fourth-generation Jews who reject both denominational and religious definitions of their Jewishness—a source of common concern to Jewish leadership in both Israel and North America. Congruent with this finding is the cross-generational relationship between outmarriage and visiting Israel. Core Jewish respondents who have two Jewish parents have a much higher rate of visiting Israel (36 percent), than the respondents who have only one parent who is Jewish, either mother (7 percent) or father (5 percent) (Table 27). The respondents with one Jewish parent most frequently reported being raised in secular homes.

Figure 9
Visits to Israel by Jewish Denomination

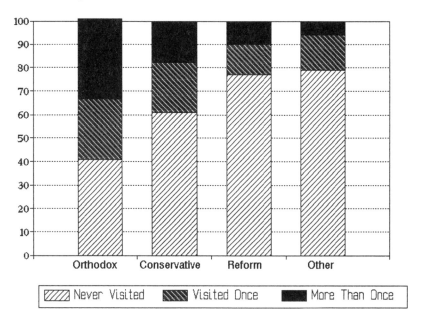

THE VISIT TO ISRAEL AND MEASURES OF JEWISH IDENTIFICATION

Is there any difference in the degree of Jewish religious practice among those respondents who have been to Israel and those who have not? The Index of Jewish Religious Practice (Table 29) was constructed by identifying elements of Jewish identity and assigning one point for each positive response. These elements included synagogue attendance, Sabbath candle lighting, participation in a Passover seder, fasting on Yom Kippur, and lighting Chanukah candles. All the items on the Jewish Religious Practice Index are correlated with visits to Israel. In Figure 10 the degree of religious practice is defined as low, medium, or high and is composed of the aggregate scores on the different items of religious practice found in Table 29. The degree of religious practice is significantly higher for those who have visited Israel once (45 percent), and even higher still for those respondents who have visited more than once (58 percent). Both of these can be compared to respondents who had never visited Israel, of whom only 23 percent earned a high score on the Index of Religious Practice. To illustrate even further, the same pattern occurs in Table 29. Respondents who have visited Israel are more likely to attend synagogue more than once a year as well as fast on Yom Kippur. Moreover, they are more likely to live in households in which someone celebrates a Passover Seder, lights Sabbath candles, lights Chanukah candles, and attends a Purim celebration. By the same token, of the respondents who had a low score on the Jewish Religious Practice Index, only 6 percent ever visited Israel compared to 44 percent of respondents with high Jewish religious practice. But given the available data, there is no way of knowing what came first, the religious practice or the visit to Israel.

Figure 10
Visits to Israel by Jewish Religious Practice Index

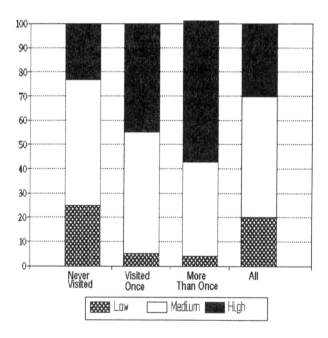

JEWISH IDENTIFICATION, THE VISIT TO ISRAEL, AND AGE

The same pattern between an Israel visit and the degree of religious practice applies within each age group, especially the young; in every age group, those who have traveled to Israel have a higher degree of religious practice than those who have not. Thus we find that even among the 18-34 year olds, 54 percent of those who have visited Israel report a high degree of Jewish religious practice as compared to only 17 percent of their peers who have never visited Israel. The same applies to the two older age groups (Figure 11). Visiting Israel is positively associated with Jewish religious practice among all ages, illustrating the salient association between the Israel experience and North American Jewish identity (Table 30).

Figure 11
Visits to Israel by Degree of Religious Practice by Age

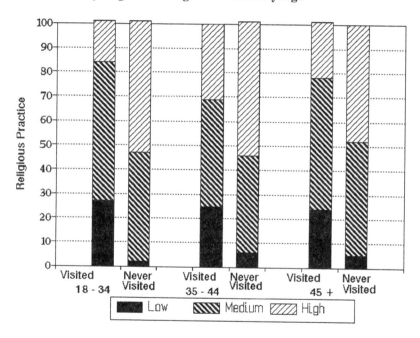

MEASURES OF JEWISH COMMUNAL AFFILIATION AND VISITS TO ISRAEL

Does a visit to Israel have any association with the degree of Jewish communal affiliation? Once again we see the pattern repeated. Similar to the Jewish Religious Practice Index, an Index of Jewish Communal Affiliation was constructed by giving one point to positive responses on each of the following items: subscribing to a Jewish periodical, affiliation in at least one Jewish organization, having close friends or family living in Israel, having mostly Jewish friends, living in a neighborhood with Jewish character, and donating to a Jewish charity in 1989. On every measure of Jewish affiliation, those who have visited Israel once have a higher affiliation score than those who have never visited Israel. However, this could also be an indication that those who are already affiliated within the Jewish community are more exposed to opportunities for visiting Israel than those who are not affiliated or whose affiliation is minimal.

Of special interest is the relationship between visits and philanthropy. Of those who have never visited Israel, only 43 percent live in households where any contribution has been made to a Jewish charity. For those who have been to Israel only once, this figure rises to 69 percent, while for those respondents who have visited Israel more than once this figure rises to 82 percent (Table 31). The philanthropic behavior might indicate a two-way relationship, as those who regularly contribute to Jewish causes are perhaps also more inclined to visit Israel.

Does this relationship change with age? The answer is that Jewish communal affiliation increases with age, but it is also strongly correlated with a visit to Israel. As can be seen in Figure 12, when considering only those people who

Figure 12
Visits to Israel by Degree of Jewish Communal Affiliation by Age

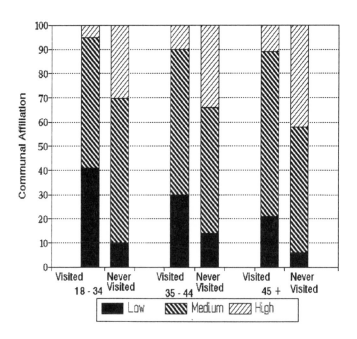

have been to Israel, older respondents have a higher degree of Jewish affiliation than younger respondents, as we would expect given the family and household basis of affiliation of American Jewry. However, the critical finding is that within each age group those who have been to Israel have a higher degree of affiliation than those who have not. Even in the 18-34 age group, while only 5 percent of those who have never been to Israel were highly affiliated, 30 percent of those who had visited Israel were highly affiliated (Table 32). It could be argued that this is merely a reflection of the type of Jewish home life of the respondents and not of their visit to Israel. In order to deal with this question we need to try at least to control for the effect of the home, represented by the variable of denomination.

JEWISH IDENTIFICATION, VISITS TO ISRAEL, AND DENOMINATION

While the degree of religious practice and communal affiliation declines as one moves from Orthodox to Reform on the denominational hierarchy, on both religious and civic measures, respondents who have been to Israel always score higher than those who have not. This is true for every denomination, including Orthodox respondents. However, a second visit to Israel is not associated with an increase in the religious practice of the Reform respondents (Table 33). As reported in Table 34, one visit to Israel is associated with a higher level of community affiliation for Reform Jews from 8 percent for those who have never visited Israel to 25 percent for those who have visited once only, while the second visit is correlated with a still higher rate, 39 percent. Similarly, Conservative Jews move from 15 percent to 29 percent, while after a second visit they increase to 60 percent high degree of communal affiliation. In sum, visiting Israel is strongly associated with more intensive Jewish civics and, to a lesser but significant degree, religious practice.

JEWISH IDENTIFICATION, THE VISIT TO ISRAEL, AND JEWISH EDUCATION

What is the relationship between Jewish education and measures of Jewish continuity? Medding et al. (1992), have shown that there is a relationship between Jewish education and rates of inmarriage (an important condition of Jewish continuity), where these differences are . . . "based on duration of Jewish education, particularly so at a younger age. . . . The association between more than six years of Jewish education and inmarriage is stronger in younger age groups" (12).

In this study we examine the relationship between the amount of Jewish education completed and measures of Jewish continuity—namely, Jewish religious practice and rates of intermarriage. In addition, we will utilize this established relationship and inmarriage to serve as a controlling baseline against which to assess the additional effect, if any, of a visit to Israel among those respondents who have had the same duration of Jewish schooling. This proposition will be tested in a more sophisticated statistical analysis offered below.

Is it at all possible to isolate the effect of a single visit to Israel on the Jewish identification of respondents? Following Medding et al., if we take the respondents who have had less than six years of Jewish education and assume that they share a similar background, we can compare the scores on the Jewish Religious Practice Index between those who have never visited Israel at all and those who have visited Israel only once. We can thereby approximate the effect of the Israel visit independent of prior Jewish schooling on the Jewish identity of participants, since Jewish schooling almost always comes before a visit to Israel, just as education predates marriage.

Since the responses obtained in NJPS reflect only one point in time, cause and effect temporal relationships can never be conclusively ascertained irrespective of the methodology. This is especially true when we do not know when the visit to Israel occurred. Nevertheless, the observation of persistent patterns of association between variables, when rigorously analyzed—namely, controlling for previsit background variables—allows us to infer, although not conclude, the grounds for causal relationships which need to be proven using other data.

Looking at Figure 13 we see the dramatic increase in Jewish religious practice between respondents with low Jewish education who have never visited Israel (23 percent) and those who have visited only once (47 percent) (Table 35). Just as important, one must note the case of all those respondents with a significant Jewish education, where the difference between visitors and nonvisitors in high index of practice ranges from 36 percent to 57 percent. Even if respondents benefit from an intense Jewish education, an Israel visit continues to reflect or to serve as an extra powerful element in the Jewish identity of the individual.

It may be argued that perhaps this relation is really a mediated outcome of the respondent's denomination. Since, as is well known, Jewish education is positively correlated with denomination, this analysis was conducted separately for the Conservative and Reform respondents, allowing us to control for denomination, as seen in Tables 36 and 37.

From these data we can see that among both Conservative and Reform Jews, the same pattern applies at almost all levels of Jewish education. Among Conservative respondents with low Jewish education, the contrast between visitors and nonvisitors on the high Jewish religious practice score ranges from 37 percent to 59 percent. At the same time, among Reform respondents it ranges from 24 percent to 38 percent (Table 37). In both denominations, though particularly among the Reform respondents, the pattern is maintained for those with high (more than six years) Jewish education.

Figure 13
Visits to Israel by Jewish Religious Practice by Jewish Education of All Core Jewish Respondents

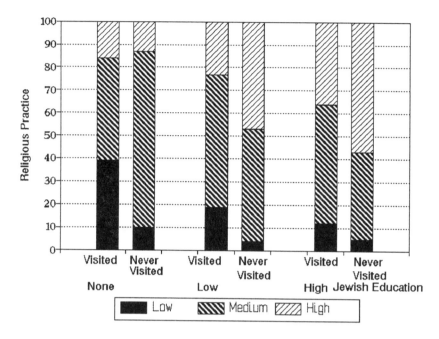

A visit to Israel seems, then, to continue to be associated with higher religious practice scores not only for those respondents who had the benefit of little or no Jewish education, but even for respondents with higher Jewish education. The pattern is maintained even among Orthodox respondents, although we might have expected it to be less because of their generally stronger Jewish education and home background.

Thus far we have applied two positive indices of Jewish behavior as measures of Jewish ethnicity to measure its relation to the Israel visit. We now turn to a third, albeit negative, measure of Jewish ethnicity, the case of outmarriage. There is no analysis offered of the rates, causes, and consequences of outmarriage, as this is not the purpose of this study. Outmarriage is used as a measure of association with the Jewish community and its life choices. Is a visit to Israel in any way associated to this life choice?

CHAPTER 9

Outmarriage

Outmarriage is a Jewish concern but not an exclusively Jewish concern. On the contrary, Kosmin and Lachman (1993) have found a rising rate of outmarriage among religious denominations in America of the 1980s and 1990s. While not all outmarriage results in a switch in religion, an overall 25-30 percent of all Americans switch religion or denomination during their lifetime and marriage is the most important reason for them doing so. Kosmin and Lachman attribute this trend to later marriage age, greater economic self-sufficiency of the partners, as well the norms of individualism and interreligious tolerance and pluralism. An indicator of the gradient of this trend can be seen in the fact that while 94 percent of Jews were living in religiously homogeneous households in 1957, this had dropped to 69 percent by the early 1990s.

Outmarriage is defined by this study as occurring whenever a core Jewish individual marries a non-Jew who does not become a Jew by choice. Table 38 tells us 36 percent of all respondents are married to a Gentile spouse who did not convert. This percentage increases among younger age cohorts. Thus, 50 percent of the respondents between the ages of 35 and 44 and 54 percent of the respondents under age 35 are currently outmarried.[1] In addition, contrary to earlier patterns, there is no longer any significant difference between the rates of outmarriage of men (37 percent) and women (35 percent) (Table 39).

OUTMARRIAGE, GENDER, AND SOCIOECONOMIC STATUS

As has been cited above, 19 percent of all core Jews are in the upper income group, although this rate varies by gender. Twenty-one percent of men as compared to 17 percent of women fall into this category. Is the relationship between income and outmarriage affected by gender? Again, it appears that high socioeconomic status is more strongly associated with inmarriage than with outmarriage, especially among young males. In fact, 25 percent of inmarried core Jews are in the upper income category compared to only 17 percent of outmarried core Jews. Further analysis reveals that Jewish women under the age of 45 who marry a non-Jew are more likely to marry down (hypogamically) than are Jewish men under the age of 45 who do the same. This is reflected in the finding that more outmarried men, 21 percent, compared to 13 percent of outmarried women are found in the $80,000 and above income group. At the same time, 23 percent of all inmarried men compared to 26 percent of inmarried women are in the same upper income category. The same pattern holds for all young Jews whether Jews by religion or secular. This finding seems to support the view that marriage market opportunities vary by gender and that it is easier for men to marry the women they prefer than vice versa (Grossbard-Schechtman, 1993:147ff). Indeed, here hypogamy would be expected to be related to socioeconomic status, especially for younger women.

THE ISRAEL VISIT AND OUTMARRIAGE

Is there a difference in the rate of outmarriage between young core Jews who have visited Israel and those who have not? Core Jewish respondents who have visited Israel were outmarried far less (15 percent) than those who have never visited (44 percent) (Table 40). In every age group those who have never visited Israel were outmarried to a much greater degree than those who had visited Israel. Thus, 18-34 year olds who have never visited reported an outmarriage rate of 62 percent while their peers who have visited Israel reported an outmarried rate of 19 percent (Figure 14). It is worth mentioning that younger Jews from lower and middle income groups are less likely to visit Israel and also less likely to marry within the Jewish community (Table 41).

The highest rates of outmarriage characterize the third and fourth generations in which 50 to 54 percent of core Jewish respondents who have never visited Israel marry non-Jews. The rate of outmarriages is lower, 22 and 36 percent, respectively, for the respondents in these generations who have visited Israel compared to the 50-54 percent outmarriage rate of those who have never visited. There is a sharp increase in the level of outmarriage between the first- and second-generation respondents who have never visited Israel, 23 percent, and the third generation of respondents who have never visited Israel, 50 percent. The level of outmarriage was significantly lower for second- and third- generation respondents who have visited Israel, 5 percent and 22 percent, respectively (Figure 15) (Table 42).

As already noted, gender appears to be a nondiscriminatory variable with respect to the rate of outmarriage From Table 43 it can be seen that the coincidence between a visit to Israel and a radical drop in the level of outmarriage is almost equal among both men and women. For male "once only visitors," the rate of outmarriage is 19 percent, while for nonvisitors it is 48

Figure 14
Frequency of Outmarriage by Age and Visit to Israel

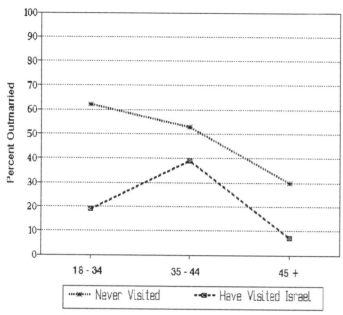

percent. Among women the outmarriage rate rises from 21 percent to 42 percent. We will test these relations further by controlling for denomination and Jewish education.

OUTMARRIAGE, THE VISIT TO ISRAEL, AND DENOMINATION

Outmarriage is least present among core Jewish respondents who are currently Orthodox, 8 percent. Conservative respondents reported a rate of 22 percent, while Reform Jews reported 36 percent. Yet within each denomination, which symbolizes a different type of Jewish education and lifestyle, the rate of outmarriage is lower by a wide margin for the respondents who have been to Israel than for those who have never visited Israel (Table 44a).

The rate of outmarriage among respondents raised as Conservative or Reform Jews is considerably higher than for those who currently define themselves respectively as Conservative or Reform (Table 44b). For those who have never visited Israel, 40 percent of those raised Conservative and 55 percent of Reform have outmarried. This rate drops by almost half on the basis of one visit to Israel to 23 percent for Conservative respondents and 28 percent for Reform Jews. The decrease in outmarriage also applies to the Orthodox community where the rate drops from 27 percent for those who have never visited to 2 percent for those who have visited more than once (Figure 16).

Figure 15
Visit to Israel by Jewish Identification of Spouse by Generation of Respondent

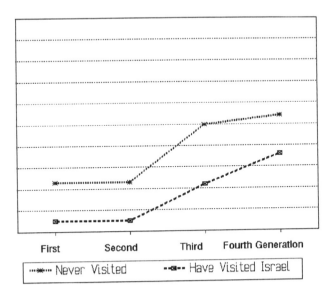

Figure 16
Frequency of Outmarriage by Visit to Israel by Denomination Raised

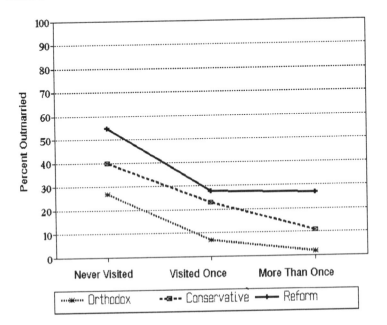

OUTMARRIAGE, THE VISIT TO ISRAEL, AND JEWISH EDUCATION

Respondents who have a strong Jewish education as defined above and who have visited Israel are the least likely to marry outside the Jewish community (10 percent) (Figure 17). This subgroup outmarries less than respondents with a low Jewish education but have never visited Israel (41 percent), or respondents with a low Jewish education and only one visit to Israel (21 percent) (Table 45). An Israel visit has an influence irrespective of the level of Jewish education the respondents have acquired. But does this pattern apply to the younger respondents whose marriage choice might have actually been more affected by a visit?

Figure 17
Frequency of Outmarriage of Core Jewish Respondents by Jewish Education by Visit to Israel

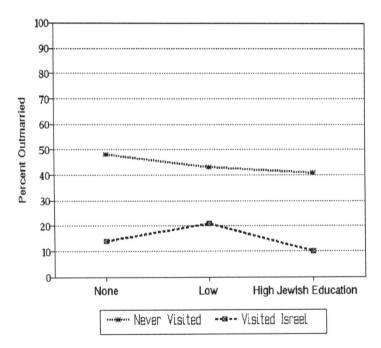

Outmarriage for people who are 45 and over is less likely among respondents who have visited Israel, no matter what level their Jewish education (Table 46). Respondents who are 45 and over who have never been to Israel but have either a low or high level of Jewish education still have a significant rate of outmarriage, 27 percent and 39 percent, respectively. However, among those who have been to Israel, the rate drops to 11 percent and 4 percent, respectively. Turning to respondents under 45 years old, we find that those with low Jewish education who had never been to Israel have a 58 percent outmarriage rate. The additional factor of a visit to Israel is associated with a lower rate, 42 percent (Figure 18). Perhaps even more startling is the finding that those with more Jewish education, namely afternoon school beyond six years, but who had never visited Israel, had an outmarriage rate of 44 percent. Those whose Jewish education background was similar but had visited Israel had only a 17 percent outmarriage rate (Table 47). It appears that a visit to Israel is not by itself a means of formal or informal socialization among American Jews, but a factor which may well serve to intensify the effect of the other agencies of socialization. It cannot and should not be expected to replace them. Yet there is good reason to expect that the visit to Israel can and often actually may contribute to the enhancement of Jewish identity among North American Jews. Moreover, it serves this function irrespective of denomination, age, or gender. However, accessibility to an Israel experience is not equally distributed throughout American Jewry. This must be recognized in programs concerned with the future of the community, its richness, stamina and vitality.

Figure 18
Frequency of Outmarriage of Core Jewish Respondents Aged 18-44 by Jewish Education by Visit to Israel

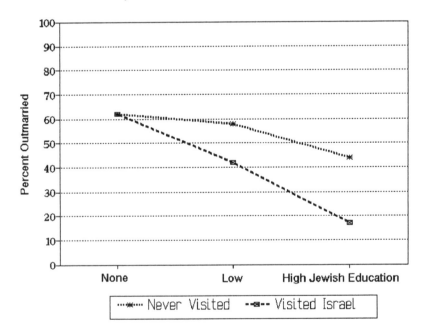

NOTE

1. The reported rate of outmarriage among individual respondents bears a relationship to the rate of outmarriage among couples. The couple rate indicates what proportion of all marriages include a non-Jewish spouse. It does not tell us the number of all Jews who currently outmarry. Nevertheless, the couple rate is a reliable descriptive measure upon which different sectors of American Jewry can be compared. The couple rate is nonetheless higher than the reported rate of outmarriage for all core Jewish adults, which is about 28 percent. This compares with the couple rate of 36 percent cited above. The standard arithmetic formula for transforming the couple rate to a respondent rate indicates that the 54 percent couple rate of outmarriage for 18-34 year olds equals a 36 percent couple rate of outmarriage (Table 38). I will, however, continue to report here only the couple rates as they reflect most authentically the NJPS sample based on household. Conversions may be calculated by the reader as desired. The formula for converting couple rate to respondent rate as follows, where:

m = % of mixed couples and m = % of out-married persons

$$m_s = \frac{m_c}{\frac{2 - m_c}{100}}$$

(Della Pergola, 1972: 141).

CHAPTER 10

The Intention to Visit Israel and the Jewishness of Respondents

Who plans to visit Israel within three years beyond the date of the survey? Sixty-four percent of all core Jews report that no one in their household had such plans. Twenty-seven percent say that someone in their household was planning to visit, while an additional 9 percent did not know. Thus slightly more households in the overall core Jewish population say they intend to visit Israel than actually report visiting. This group constitutes a key potential market for those wishing to encourage travel to Israel. Who constitutes this group?

Unfortunately, we do not really know the answer to this question since respondents were questioned about members of their household rather than themselves specifically. What, then, can we derive from this data? To begin with, among Jews by religion who have already been to Israel, 42 percent belong to households containing a member who plans to visit. By contrast, among respondents who have not visited, only 22 percent were members of households in which anyone intended to visit in the next three years (Table 48). What type of self-definition of Jewishness characterizes respondents who report on these intentions, and may we infer something about the intenders themselves?

Seven percent of all core Jewish households where respondents have never visited include Jews by choice, yet a high proportion of these households have members who plan to visit Israel (Table 48). Among respondents who have never visited, 45 percent of Jews by choice report plans to visit Israel by some household member within three years after the survey date, which is more than double the rate of Jews by religion (22 percent) who have never visited. A much smaller rate was reported by ethnic-secular households, out of whom a mere 8 percent reported plans to visit Israel in the next three years (Table 48) At the same time, intentions are greater for Jews by Religion and Jews by

Choice among those who have already visited. It seems clear that visiting Israel is associated with other measures of Jewish identification, especially a prior visit. One visit leads to another, while the interplay between background and visit has different consequences for different Jews (Table 48).

The central finding about the relationship between denomination and intention to visit, seen in Table 49, lies in the relatively small difference between Conservative and Reform households. Indeed, among households where respondents report having never visited Israel, 26 percent of Reform compared to 20 percent of Conservative report plans to visit Israel in the next three years. Among those who have already visited Israel, 39 percent of Reform respondents compared to 36 percent of Conservative respondents report someone in household has plans to visit again. Among Orthodox households, 88 percent of those who have visited Israel report plans to visit in the next three years. Because there are not enough single-person households in the survey to support an analysis based upon them, it is important to realize that it is not necessarily the respondent who will visit, but any member of his or her household. The data here are revealing since it is the Reform households which constitute an untapped source of visitors that is larger than all other non-Orthodox respondents who have never been to Israel.

To what extent is intention to visit Israel affected by degree of Jewish education? From Table 50 we can see that in line with earlier findings, in the same hierarchical decreasing order, visitors and those intending to visit Israel have had more Jewish education than their peers who do not. It is important to note, however, that among households where the respondent has never visited but planned to visit, 65 percent had only a low Jewish education. Thus, when determining the Israel Experience target population for policy purposes, there is a clear demarcation point between those with a low Jewish education and those who had none. Purveyors of the Israel Experience might consider engaging that relatively untapped area of the market formed by Jews with a low level of Jewish education before trying to reach those without any Jewish education at all.

What is the relationship between age and intention to visit Israel? Important to note in Table 51 is that while 18 percent of respondents aged 18-34 who have never visited Israel report that someone in their household intends to do so, only 14 percent of the 35-44 year olds report similar plans. This would indicate that a major effort should be invested in this younger age category, especially if programmatic goals include intensifying Jewish behavior and strengthening Jewish identity. In addition, it is clear that the households of respondents in the 18-34 age group are a primary target for the second visits to Israel. While, as we have seen above, this sector comprises only 21 percent of all prior visitors, 51 percent of this age group report that someone in their household intends to visit Israel again in the next three years, compared to 44 percent of the 35-44 age group.

It again needs to be stressed that, although this analysis rests on a tenuous overidentification between respondent and household, it has importance for the pattern it reflects. No firm conclusions may be drawn from the relationship between personal data and intention to visit. This problem does not exist, however, for the broad categories such as income or region, which properly define households and are discussed below.

MARITAL STATUS AND THE INTENTION TO VISIT ISRAEL

The responses of never married singles offer the only opportunity to isolate the relationship between a prior visit and "intention", simply because the "intention" reported by all other respondents may reflect anticipated behavior of anyone in the household. Twenty-two percent of core Jews reported still being single (Table 52); within this group 26 percent report the intention to visit Israel in the next few years, a far higher response than among any other category. In the case of marrieds, for example, only 19 percent who have never visited report the intention of doing so within the next three years. This finding argues for a radical initiative to help singles realize this intention before they make their marriage choice and settle down. This idea is discussed further in the conclusion of this book (Chapter 13 below).

REGION AND THE INTENTION TO VISIT ISRAEL

Within every region, the percentage of intenders increases considerably with a prior visit. For example, in the densely Jewish Northeast, which makes up 40 percent of the households of the core Jewish population whose respondents have never visited Israel, 21 percent report an intention to visit. Among Northeast households that do report a visit, 41 percent report another visit planned in the next three years. In the Midwest, which comprises 7 percent of the population, only 14 percent of its never visited households report the intention to visit, in comparison to 34 percent for those who have visited. The South, whose percentage of first-time intenders reflects its proportion of the population, namely 25 percent, demonstrates the highest rate by far of intention to visit. Among Southerners who have visited Israel once, the intention to visit rate is 43 percent. Finally, in the Western region, where the proportion of first-time intenders is lower than its proportion of the population (18 percent), we again find that in households where respondents have visited Israel, a much higher percentage (39 percent) report an intention to visit in the next three years (Table 53).

INCOME AND INTENTION

Income seems to positively influence intention, especially for those who have never been to Israel. In the lowest and middle income categories, only 16 and 19 percent, respectively, of those who have never visited Israel report the intention to do so. By contrast, in the highest income category of $80,000 or more, a full 33 percent report the intention to visit Israel in the next three years (Table 54). This suggests that the cost of a trip to Israel, analogous to the cost of Jewish education, is too high for many potential first-time single and other visitors. Ironically, a trip to Israel may be the only form of Jewish education some individuals ever receive. In households where Jews have already been to Israel, income appears to be less of a barrier. We find that in both lower and middle income categories 50 percent of the households whose respondents had been to Israel report the intention to visit in the next three years. As noted earlier, with regard to tourism in general, visiting friends and relatives makes a prospective visit less income elastic or less sensitive to changes in income of the prospective traveler. Visits to Israel, which are often centered around a pilgrimage, a family visit, or professional conference, should be more immune to economic instability. Indeed, for low-income groups the rate of intention to visit Israel is significantly higher than among respondents in the highest income category. For those who have never been to Israel, the exact opposite obtains. Only high-income households report the intention of a first visit to Israel.

Since age and income are known to be directly correlated, it is no surprise that in the NJPS data 49 percent of respondents aged 18 to 34 fall within the lowest income group. Is there any difference in the rate of intention to visit Israel among younger low-income households between those who have already visited Israel and those who have not? The module data subsample is very small for these respondents, but relying on only the youngest cohort in the lowest income group, we see that among those who have never visited Israel only 7 percent report that someone in their household intends to do so. Among respondents who have visited Israel, 57 percent report that someone in their household intends to visit Israel within the next three years.

This leads to the conclusion that low income can be a serious detriment to recruiting first-time visitors, so that subsidies probably should be restricted to those people who have never been to Israel before. Having been to Israel at least one time, it seems, brings about a restructuring of priorities such that individuals are more likely to find the resources for their next visit.

INTENTION AND IMPACT: A FINAL LOOK

In Tables 33 and 34, we compared the Jewish identity scores of those who had actually been to Israel with those who had not. We discerned a wide gap between visitors and nonvisitors and inferred with caution that this difference is attributable, at least in part, to the visit itself. Thereafter, we proceeded to examine this relationship in a more stringent fashion by controlling successively for a long series of variables which could be reasonably hypothesized to account, alternatively, for all or most of this difference. In any one of these analyses, the effect of a visit to Israel might have appeared insignificant. This did not occur in a single case; rather a clear pattern of association persisted throughout.

Steve Cohen (1992b), from his analysis of his data on Canadian Jewish youth, infers the impact of an Israel visit on different indices of Jewish identity. As we have noted, many of the differences between visitors and nonvisitors are the result of processes which occurred prior to the respondent's first trip to Israel rather than because of the trip itself. Cohen's research indicates that when first-time visitors are compared with nonvisitors who intend to visit Israel within the next three years, the intenders' scores on indices of Jewish identity resemble those of first-time visitors prior to their first visit. Therefore, differences found between those who have visited Israel once and those who have not but intend to do appear to be attributable to the effect of the visit.

Tables 55 and 56 offer the opportunity to compare core Jews who report the intention to visit Israel, but have not yet done so, with those who have already visited but only once, classified by their degree of religious practice and their level of communal affiliation. We find that on both indices of Jewish identification, religious and civic, it is reasonable to infer that a higher index score is positively related to an Israel visit. Thus, 74 percent of those have visited once who report a household intention to visit again show a high score on the religious practice index compared to 30 percent of those who have never been to Israel but reported the intention to in the next three years. Turning to the civic index presented in Table 56, we find that 51 percent of one-time visitors have a high score as compared to only 34 percent of the never visited who reported the intention to do so. Obviously the small numbers who have visited more than once have still higher scores on both indices.

However, there is another story within the tables. Respondents who have visited Israel once, but report no one in their household with the intention of doing so within the next three years, score only marginally better on both indices, if at all, than intenders who have never been to Israel. They do, however, receive higher scores than those who have never visited Israel nor ever intend to.

Respondents who have visited Israel and score high on Jewish religious practice are also more likely to intend to visit Israel again within three years. Those who do not intend to revisit tend to score lower on the Jewish Religious Practice Index. This implies, although not demonstrated conclusively here, that in order to sustain a higher score on both indices of Jewish identification than those who have never been to Israel at all, one's first visit must be good enough to generate the intention to visit again within three years.

With regard to the content and quality of the visits, the 1990 NJPS sheds little light. We do, however, gain some insight into what constitutes a quality Israel visit from Cohen and Wall's recent report "Excellence in Youth Trips to Israel" (1994: 15-17). The elements they list include:

1. Consideration for the age of the participants and placing the experience in the appropriate framework for participating children and youth.

2. A particular goal or philosophy which is expressed through a "curriculum" in the sense of it being a set of guiding contents, values, and ideas. It is not simply an "itinerary" or schedule of events. It is a carefully woven scenario which reflects a world view.
3. Both formal and informal educational experiences which might include meeting Israelis, shopping in a supermarket, or sipping coffee in a Tel Aviv cafe. These experiences can be as enlightening as a formal lecture.
4. Quality educators, counselors, and guides.
5. A good group experience based on the sharing and exchanging of ideas.
6. An educational component both prior to and following the trip.

The Israel visit should not be a singular event in one's Jewish experience, but rather one of the many aspects of an ongoing Jewish education. Additional trips to Israel only intensify the participant's level of Jewish identification.

CHAPTER 11

The Impact of the Israel Visit on Jewish Identity: A Comprehensive Parametric Analysis of the NJPS Data

THE ANALYTICAL MODEL

In the analysis of earlier chapters it has been possible to determine an association between visiting Israel and indices of Jewish religious practice and Jewish communal affiliation, each of which reflects a different cultural segment of Jewish identity. However, this form of analysis is limited by the fact that it is impossible to know which association among many is the more powerful one in explaining the differences between respondents on their scores for Jewish religious practice and Jewish communal affiliation. It is often argued, of course, that the real or effective explanation of both visits to Israel *and* Jewish religious practice is Jewish schooling or denomination or both, so that in fact the Israel visit actually has no independent weight of its own. The following analysis places the visit to Israel in direct competition with alternative explanations for the behavior that is being examined. If indeed the visit to Israel has no independent contribution to make to the explanation of variance in, for example, Jewish religious practice, it is to be expected that its weight will be statistically insignificant when controlling for the alternative independent variables.

What are the alternative variables? The analyses that follow utilize four models in which the independent variables and the covariates are the same; where the analysis is performed concurrently with two different dependent variables: Jewish Religious Practice Index and Jewish Communal Affiliation Index; as well as on two different population sets: the core Jewish population and the core population with both parents Jewish. The additional independent variables include Jewish education and denomination, which are regarded as correlates for previsit levels of measures of Jewish identification, as well as outmarriage status and age. This analysis is performed while controlling for the socioeconomic variables of household income, educational attainment, and gender of the respondents. At the theoretical level the hypothesis is that if the association between visit to Israel and the dependent variables is still significant as indicated in column 7 of the following tables, this will mean that it is significant even when taking into account the weight of Jewish education, the denomination of the respondent, the current age of the respondent, and even whether the respondent is currently single, never-married, or, if outmarried, irrespective of respondents' educational attainment, household income and gender of respondent.

In order to determine the relative weight of the variables (1) visit to Israel, (2) Jewish education, (3) denomination, (4) age, and (5) outmarriage status on the two indices of Jewish identification (Jewish religious practice and communal affiliation) when controlled for (a) educational attainment, (b) income and (c) gender, a multiple classification analysis was performed. This procedure requires some preliminary clarification.

The analysis that follows (Tables 57-60, 65, 66) utilizes several measures of association. The first is the correlation statistic, or ratio, *eta*. Eta is associated with the set of unadjusted category effects for each factor in the multiple classification analysis table. The square of eta indicates the proportion of variance explained by a given factor, all categories considered. In each table the dependent variable has a range from 0 - 1 and the grand mean of the variable is cited at the top of the table.

In Table 57 the dependent variable is the Jewish Religious Practice Index. The independent variables are visit to Israel, Jewish education, denomination, age and outmarriage status of the respondent. From column 2, we can immediately see the change in the raw score of the dependent variable for each category of the independent variable. For example, respondents who have never visited Israel score five points less than the grand mean on the Religious Practice Index. Those who have visited Israel only once score eight points higher, and those who have visited Israel more than once score 16 points higher. This measure of association is also reflected in the size of the eta score of .28.

In a similar fashion we can observe the positive association between Jewish education and denomination with Jewish religious practice as well as the lack of association between age and this same index. With respect to marital status, which compares never-marrieds, inmarrieds, and outmarrieds in order to control for the outmarriage effect, inmarried respondents scored higher on the dependent variable than both never-marrieds and outmarrieds. The key question is whether the positive association between visiting Israel and Jewish religious practice is sustained when controlling for all the other factors in the equation, separately and together, including Jewish education, denomination, age, and outmarriage status. Furthermore, is it also maintained when controlling for the covariates, namely, educational attainment, household income, and the gender of the respondent?

The answer to this question is found in the changes in the raw scores, columns 2, 4 and 6, as well as in the changes of the beta scores, columns 5 and 7. It is evident that visit to Israel is consistently associated with Jewish religious practice, since the beta score when adjusted for the factors alone is .17 and when adjusted for the independent variables and the covariates as well is .15.[1] Looking at the entire table we see that the single most important determinant is, somewhat surprisingly, not the background variable of denomination. The two variables which have equal but independent weight are visit to Israel and Jewish education. Age is the weakest variable of all, while being inmarried not surprisingly shows a strong positive association with Jewish religious practice. Overall, 29 percent of the variance in the dependent variable is explained by this equation in which visit to Israel makes its own independent contribution to that explanation. This score is considered high by social science standards.

The clear finding here is that the association between the Israel visit and Jewish religious practice is definitively not a spurious correlation nor a mere reflection of other background variables such as Jewish education or denomination. That is to say, there is a correlation between the visits to Israel and Jewish religious practice independent of past Jewish education and so on. This now indeed supports the hypothesis that whatever background the respondent has come from, an Israel visit makes it more likely that they would have a higher score on Jewish religious practice. The absence of time sequence makes causal conclusions impossible but the weight of the Israel visit independent of other background variables must now be acknowledged.

Once again it needs to be emphasized that since this analysis deals with only cross-sectional data, cause-effect cannot be conclusively inferred; however, the analysis does provide an opportunity to give the best approximation of competing explanations for the variance in indices of Jewish identity and the probable weight that the visit to Israel has. This should not be surprising since for example, the older Jewish youth are when they first visit Israel, the more likely it is that the Israel visit is to be independent of home, denomination, and Jewish schooling. Indeed, previous research has already told us that among college-age first timers as high as 25 percent of first-time visitors to Israel have little or no Jewish schooling at all.

Table 58 repeats the same model of analysis as in Table 57, but the dependent variable is the Index of Jewish Affiliation. Here the grand mean is .39, a far lower score for the entire population than that of the Jewish Religious Practice Index. This score indicates that Jews report a lower rate of affiliation than of Jewish ritual practice. The variable which contributes most to an increase in the raw score of Jewish affiliation is visit to Israel (eta .41). Moreover, this strong association is maintained when controlling for the other factors, as indicated by the beta score of .28, as well as when controlling for all the covariates resulting in a beta score of .26. However, this association is not necessarily exclusive, since prior affiliation may help to explain an Israel visit. Looking at the other factors in the equation, we see that low Jewish education makes no contribution to Jewish affiliation, while strong Jewish education makes only a small contribution (5 deviation points). Orthodox Jews are highly affiliated, followed by Conservative Jews. Being Reform and "just Jewish" has negative consequences for general Jewish affiliation. There is a linear relationship between age and affiliation, however. Only those aged 45 and over have a Jewish affiliation score higher than the mean. The same is true for people who are inmarried. What is striking is that the equation contributes 36 percent of the explanation of the variance in the dependent variable, a high figure in such cases, where visit to Israel is a dominant factor. This strongly suggests that visit to Israel is very positively associated with being affiliated with the with the Jewish community.

In order to maximize our ability to control for the Jewishness of the home, it is important to ask whether these relationships hold when we examine core Jews with two Jewish parents In the two following analyses (Tables 59 and 60) we hold constant antecedent variables related to Jewishness of the household which may perhaps account for differences among the respondents that would not be immediately self-evident. For the most part, the pattern of findings presented in Table 59 are similar to those discussed above regarding the weight of visit to Israel, Jewish education, and denomination in explaining the variance in the degree of Jewish religious practice. While the initial scores are higher with respondents from inmarried Jewish homes, the adjusted beta for visit to Israel is a high .23. Interestingly enough, we see from the age variable that youth here is positively (though weakly) associated with the dependent variable Jewish religious practice, in contrast with the analysis summarized in Table 57. This means that not all core Jewish youth score lower on Jewish religious practice. Core Jewish youth with two Jewish parents are more likely to score higher on Jewish religious practice than those with only one Jewish parent.

Turning now to the analysis of Jewish communal affiliation, in Table 60 we see that the patterns observed earlier persist. Respondents with two Jewish parents actually have a slightly higher grand mean on Jewish affiliation (.41). Visit to Israel, Jewish education, denomination, and age are all linearly associated with Jewish affiliation. The multiple R here is .47, a high score which suggests that second-generation inmarrieds have strong Jewish affiliations and that this characteristic is the combined outcome of the respondent's scores on denomination, Jewish education, and visit to Israel, as well as the inmarriage of the respondents themselves.

Summing up thus far, the clear finding presented above in the first model repeats itself in the relationship between Israel visit and Jewish affiliation. The further stricter application of these two models, by controlling for inmarriage of the parents of respondents, does not in any way alter the pattern of relationships or in any way weaken or dissolve the independent weight of the visit to Israel on these measures of Jewish identification.

DUAL IDENTITY HOUSEHOLDS

Goldstein (1992) has observed the degree to which the non-Jewish practice of having a Christmas tree has entered Jewish households. According to him, 62 percent of all core Jews never have a Christmas tree, 28 percent always or usually do, and 10 percent sometimes do. Breaking this down further, he finds that among Jews by Religion, 72 percent never observe the custom of a Christmas tree. The same is true for only 25 percent of secular Jews and 51 percent of Jews by Choice (173). As we will see below, observance of the Christmas tree custom is related to whether the respondent has a Jewish spouse or not. Considerable attention is paid here to the practice of having a Christmas tree not because of its doctrinal importance, but because it serves here as an index of the ambivalent, or at the very least ambiguous, attitude toward being Jewish and Jewish meaning.

Goldstein's finding is not surprising since, as he himself points out, a third of the households in NJPS are of mixed composition. In addition, secular Jews have a higher rate of current and parental outmarriage, as noted above, which in turn contributes to their higher rate of Christmas tree observance. Of special interest when examining the dual-identity thesis of Medding et al. (1992) is the overlap between Jewish ritual practices and Christmas tree observance. Returning to Berger and Luckman's theory (1967), we recall that individuals choose from a variety of options in the formation of their own ethnic identity. Thus, Jews choose which elements of their religion and which aspects of Jewish community life are the most salient, meaningful, and attractive to them. They are not required to choose all or nothing. This fits in neatly with Berger's analysis of the structure of American identity, which states that a pluralistic personality is formed by a combination of choices that coexist independently rather than coalesce to form a homogenous ethnic identity.

Goldstein has documented the concurrent practice of having a Christmas tree, lighting Chanukah candles, and attending a Passover seder. "Thirty percent of all mixed households always or usually have both a Christmas tree and light Chanukah candles. . . . [M]ixed religious composition quite often involves mixed religious practices," (137). Even when looking at Jews by Religion, one sees that 70 percent attend a Passover seder and light Chanukah candles, while 21 percent observe the Christmas tree custom. In addition, ritual practices such as lighting Chanukah candles or having a Christmas tree are much more common in households where young children are present. Symbolic religiosity becomes a cultural option for dual-identity households in an age where religious conversion occurs primarily in cases of intermarriage in order either to maintain family cohesiveness and/or lessen the chances for identity confusion among offspring. Thus, symbolic religiosity can be a practical solution for couples who do not wish to make a formal religious conversion (Gans, 1994:587).

Gans discusses a "Jewish objects culture" consisting of Jewish religious and secular objects which are used as tools of Jewish symbolic religiosity in order to enhance or provide content to Jewish life. Likewise, it can be added here that the Christmas tree is a religious symbol which is often "consumed" in a family or household context without religious worship. As both Gans and I have pointed out, there is found among American Jews a continuum of religious practice, hence there are people who are outmarried yet maintain a medium level of Jewish religious practice. We can now understand this to be an expression of symbolic religiosity in an increasingly home-centered religion. Thus, participation in a Passover seder expresses symbolic participation in a Jewish holiday and may fulfill the same role as the Christmas tree for the non-Jewish member of the household without either partner necessarily participating in church or synagogue.

What then is the relationship between having a Christmas tree, the Jewish Religious Practice Index and visit to Israel? From Tables 61a and 61b we see that for Jews by Religion, the practice of having a Christmas tree and Jewish religious practice show a high inverse correlation; 72 percent never observe the Christmas tree custom. On the other hand, of those Jews by Religion who have observed the Christmas tree custom, 67 percent scored medium on Jewish Religious Practice and an additional 15 percent scored higher. This outcome is a result of the fact that the Christmas tree practice should more appropriately be attributed to a household than to an individual respondent, similar to lighting candles.

The same inverse correlation is even more powerful for Jews by Religion whose parents are Jewish, though even here the overlap persists. Among all secular respondents, only 25 percent never have had a Christmas tree, though among respondents whose both parents are Jewish, the percentage that never observe the Christmas tree custom rises to 38 percent (Table 61b). These respondents have a higher, albeit medium, score on Jewish religious practice than the remainder, who have observed the Christmas tree custom. However, even among secular respondents who had observed the Christmas tree custom, 37 percent reported a medium or high score on Jewish religious practice compared to 41 percent for secular respondents whose both parents are Jewish. This means that there is no all or nothing nor mutually exclusive pattern. Both secular Jews and Jews by Religion are capable of receiving a medium score on Jewish religious practice and observing the Christmas tree custom.

Is, as Goldstein would have it, the pattern of overlap eliminated when we control for the outmarriage status of respondents? To answer this question we examine the responses of singles and inmarried only, in order to observe whether there is any overlap between Jewish religious practice and Christmas tree observance.

Looking first at Jews by Religion we find in Table 62a that the rate of never observing Christmas tree custom rises to 81 percent if the respondent is single and 89 percent if he or she is inmarried. Yet even among the very small percent of respondents who do observe the Christmas tree custom, 70 percent still receive at least a medium score on Jewish religious practice. This indicates that having a Christmas tree does not mean the exclusion of all Jewish religious practices.

What then of secular inmarried and singles? Among the secular as among the Jews by Religion, inmarrieds have a higher rate of never having a Christmas tree (36 percent) than do singles (26 percent) (Table 62b). While none of the respondents predictably are found in the highest range of Jewish religious practice, 38 and 46 percent, respectively, of Christmas tree observers do report a middle or higher range score on Jewish religious practice.

The thought arises that mixed observance is derived from outmarriage at the level of the respondents parents—that is to say, respondents who are themselves children of mixed marriages. In Table 63 we examine this question by repeating the exact same analysis in the module subsample. This includes only those single or inmarried respondents with two Jewish parents, thereby excluding the impact of mixed parentage.

With regard to Jews by Religion, there is no significant difference in the incidence of observance of Christmas tree custom when controlling for Jewish parentage and current outmarriage status. The rates of Christmas tree nonobservance of the 81 percent of Jewish by religion singles and 89 percent of inmarrieds (Table 62a), may be compared to the similar rates of 81 and 93 percent, respectively, of respondents of joint Jewish parentage, who have never had a Christmas tree. At the same time among secular respondents of joint Jewish parentage, 38 percent have never had Christmas tree compared to 25 percent among all secular respondents (Table 61b). This seems indicative of at least two things. First, being secular alone is not, ipso facto, being Christian; however, marriage to a Christian often introduces the Christmas tree into the household where it is shared by all (adults and children) within it. Herein is formed the dual-identity household.

What is most interesting is that Jewish by Religion single respondents of joint Jewish parentage who have observed the Christmas tree custom retain a higher score on Jewish religious practice (34 percent) than the overall population of Jews by Religion, as seen in Table 61a. At the same time, current inmarried Jews of joint Jewish parentage have a higher score on religious practice (54 percent), than do all Jews by Religion (45 percent). We see the retention of Jewish religious practice across inmarried generations, but by extension we can extrapolate negatively to the next generation, which will be based upon a higher percent of outmarried households. The small percent of second generation, singles, or inmarrieds that have a Christmas tree do not necessarily drop the degree of Jewish religious practice they have, but tend to incorporate it within their personal repertoire of religious practice.

Christmas tree observance thus becomes an additional, and not a contradictory, segment of one's American Jewish cultural identity. The custom tends to be adopted by those who see it as a legitimate option within their household, anticipate it later in their lifetime (singles), or observe it among siblings, other relations, or close friends. It is one of the characteristic phenomena of the increasing number of North American dual-identity households. The dual- identity household and the Christmas tree is becoming a more common rather than exceptional practice.

RELIGIOUS PRACTICE AND THE ISRAEL VISIT

How does a visit to Israel in any way influence this growing pattern of modern Jewish expression? While not able to infer direct causality, it seems that among Jews by Religion there exists a degree of displacement of one custom by the other. In Table 64a we see that among those respondents who have been to Israel, 10 percent have ever had a Christmas tree, compared to 36 percent among those who have never visited Israel. Looking at the data inversely, we find that among those who have never observed the Christmas tree custom, 39 percent have visited Israel compared to only 11 percent of Christmas tree observers.

Turning to all secular Jews, 75 percent of whom, as shown above, have ever had a Christmas tree, we find that 61 percent of those who have visited Israel have ever observed the Christmas tree custom, compared to 77 percent of those who have never visited Israel (Table 64b). Thus, while a great deal of caution must be applied here since the number of secular respondents visiting Israel is so low, it seems that the pattern of displacement is likewise found here. Similarly and more impressively, among secular respondents, both of whose parents are Jewish and who have visited Israel, 57 percent have never had a Christmas tree. A visit to Israel, as suggested by these findings, either helps to establish or reflects a more unambiguous Jewish identity among *both* religious and secular respondents.

Utilizing once again the analytical tool of multiple classification analysis, it is possible to summarize our discussion of the dual-identity household. The data are presented separately for Jews by Religion in Table 65 and secular Jews in Table 66. In this model, the closer the mean score on the dependent variable is to 1, the higher the level of Christmas tree observance and hence the stronger the level of ambivalence. The analysis suggests an inverse model of unambiguous Jewish identity, where Christmas tree observance is taken as a sign of ambiguity or ambivalence. Variables in the table that have a negative sign are forces that work against Christmas tree observance.

Looking only at Jews by Religion in Table 65, we discern a clear trend. First, as has already been demonstrated, outmarriage status is powerfully and positively associated with Christmas tree observance in dual-religion households while being never-married is not. With regard to age, only those 45 and over are negatively associated with outmarriage. Younger groups through the age of 44 are positively associated with Christmas tree observance, as indeed with outmarriage itself.

Identification of Jews as Orthodox and Conservative is negatively associated with Christmas tree observance. Being identified as a Reform Jew is positively associated on the raw score (column 2), but this becomes zero when controlling for other variables. What then of Jewish education and the visit to Israel? On the raw score, only high Jewish education seems to displace Christmas tree observance. Low Jewish education—that is, afternoon school for less than six years—plays but a neutral role. When controlling for other variables, a low score on Jewish education offers displacement of one point.

The salience of a visit to Israel is readily apparent. Only one visit to Israel on the raw score displaces Christmas tree observance by 9 points, while more than one visit does so by 11 points (column 2). This margin is reduced when controlling for all other variables, including outmarriage, to 4 points (column 4), resulting in an overall beta score of .09 (column 7).

Outmarriage is the most powerful determinant of ambivalent Jewish household identity and a Christmas tree; second to this is age. A visit to Israel is the third factor according to weight, although it works in the opposite direction, serving to displace the degree of Christmas tree observance. Following the influence of visit to Israel come the two remaining variables, denomination and Jewish education. These latter two variables, as been demonstrated by the author elsewhere (Mittelberg, 1992), are highly interrelated.

The small sample of secular Jews in NJPS limits the power of statistical analysis represented in Table 66. Still, we see that the Israel visit maintains its pattern of negative displacement by 3 points on the raw score (column 2). The patterns for Jewish education, age, denomination, and outmarriage status persist in the same directions as in the case of Jews by Religion. Noteworthy is the fact that single secular Jews are associated with Christmas tree observance, in the same way as are single Jews by Religion. In general, secular Jews with a strong Jewish education and denominational identification are less likely to have a Christmas tree than those who do not.

In summarizing both these tables, a pattern of negative association between visiting Israel and having a Christmas tree in one's home is observable. This pattern provides strong empirical evidence to support the thesis that a visit to Israel is associated with unambiguous Jewish identification and the rejection of non-Jewish symbols. Visitors to Israel seem more likely to affirm being Jewish and nothing else, rather than Jewish and something else, irrespective of whether that Jewishness is defined as religious or secular.

Much attention has been given hitherto to the segmentation of contemporary modern culture and inter alia the ethnicity of American Jews who live within it. This analysis has sought to argue that whatever the degree of pluralization or the multifariousness of segmentation, whatever the constellation of segments or the differential weights accorded to each and every one of them, whatever the ideological content of these segments, denominational, Zionist, non-Zionist, secular, religious—Jewish continuity calls for an unambiguous core of being Jewish which encompasses the household however defined. Thus, the household itself must serve as the unit of analysis for sound predictions about the quality and continuity of American Jewish life in the twenty-first century. The analysis in this chapter gives support to the hypothesis that the connection between Israel and American Jews could well be a factor contributing to the displacement of ambiguity about being a modern Jew in America.

NOTE

1. Beta is a statistic associated with the adjusted category effects for each factor. More specifically, beta is a standardized regression coefficient in the sense used in multiple regression. Finally, the Multiple R appears at the bottom of the MCA table. Just as in multiple regression, this R can be squared to indicate the variance in the dependent variable "accounted for" or explained by all independent factors and covariates.

CHAPTER 12

The Israel Connection and American Jews: Being Jewish in America in the Year 2000: Will Visiting Israel Make a Difference?

This chapter offers a unique comparison on identical dimensions of measures of Jewish identity using three data sets and two methodologies. The data sets from the National Jewish Population survey and the New York Jewish Population survey share the same basic cross-sectional methodology. Here the comparison serves primarily to cross-validate the other study's findings. A third set, relying on longitudinal data, introduces the second methodology, which extends our understanding of the impact of the Israel visit beyond what has been hitherto possible in ascertaining cause and effect. The findings are based on a follow-up study of alumni of Otzma, a one-year Israel-based work-study program. Each year, questionnaires were administered at the beginning, during, and at the conclusion of the program. Follow-up questionnaires were also distributed in North America five years after the program began. In the analysis that follows, all comparisons between data sets are limited to the answers of survey respondents between the ages of 18 and 29, the age of the Otzma alumni.

Long-term Israel experience programs have a long history, though as we have seen from Tables 1, 2a, and 2b they include only 19 percent of all participants in Israel programs. That is because most Israel programs for foreign youth are short-term summer programs intended for high school students, while the relatively few long-term programs are almost exclusively the domain of post-high school young adults. The majority of the latter are affiliated with the various Zionist youth movements such as Habonim, Bnei Akiva, Beitar, Netzer, and Young Judea, as well as certain Orthodox yeshivot.

These college-age and post-college-age programs can be divided into two principle types. The first type of program is offered through the overseas department of Israel's universities and provides participants with the opportunity to earn college credits. In principal, it operates no differently than any year-abroad program for college students. A second type of program geared to this age group may place an equal emphasis on educational goals, but offers no college credits; it involves both formal and informal study, and generally includes a significant volunteer component which is intended to integrate participants among Israelis. Among these are Machon Pardes, WUJS Arad, Sherut Le'Am, Livnot U'Lehibanot, Otzma, and Project Oren-Kibbutz Institutes for Jewish Experience.

Irrespective of their relative differences, all of these programs provide well-organized educational experiences and have accumulated evidence concerning their effectiveness, though for the most part the data were not accumulated in any systematic manner. One exception is Project Oren, the kibbutz-based semester program, which has amassed a database drawn from participant evaluations and which has been analyzed longitudinally by Mittelberg and Lev-Ari (1995).

The following analysis deals with only the year-long Otzma program of which the author has served as principal program evaluator for the past ten years. Otzma has been systematically evaluated from its beginnings and throughout all of its developmental stages. This includes a follow-up study of the program's alumni in North America five years after the program began, from which data used in this analysis was taken. The Otzma program is the only one which recruits the college aged exclusively from North America, although it offers no academic credit.

OTZMA: AN ISRAEL EXPERIENCE PROGRAM

Project *Otzma* (the name denotes both strength and courage in Hebrew) was established by the Israeli Forum in partnership with the Council of Jewish federations and participating Federations throughout North America. Otzma is a ten-month program designed to offer Jewish adults ages 18-24 an opportunity to live and volunteer in Israel in a variety of social settings, each lasting for a period of two to three months. Since its inception in 1986, approximately six hundred young adults from throughout North America have participated. Otzma aspires to excellence in the field of college-age Israel Experience programming. A discussion of the criteria for establishing excellence in youth trips to Israel is found in Cohen and Wall (1994). As part of the effort to meet these criteria, the Otzma year is divided into distinct programmatic components, each designed to give participants the opportunity to serve in various Israeli environments.

Kibbutz Ulpan

Otzma participants, known as Otzmanikim, spend the first three months living, volunteering, and studying Hebrew on kibbutz in order to acquire the language skills necessary for work in Israel. During this period, they are also integrated into many of the aspects of kibbutz life. While living on the kibbutz they also take part in weekly educational activities focused on Judaism, contemporary Israel, and the exploration of Jewish identity and values. These formal and informal educational components are supplemented by trips throughout the country which help the volunteers gain familiarity with Israel and its people. The program encourages the participants to develop their own ideas about Israeli society and the issues it faces. Many participants make strong connections with their adoptive kibbutz families or other kibbutz members and remain in contact with them even after leaving the kibbutz.

Aliyat Hanoar

During the second period of the program, participants are given their first opportunity to work independently. The Aliyat Hanoar program takes place in boarding schools throughout the country. Otzmanikim work in Hebrew with children who have learning disabilities or other special needs. Work on this track includes tutoring students and assisting instructors as well as planning and implementing social, educational, and cultural activities for the on-site population.

The Arava Track

This track gives participants an opportunity to volunteer in the agricultural sphere on Israeli collective settlements, moshavim and kibbutzim, and experience "pioneering" in the Arava desert.

Project Renewal

During the final phase of Project Otzma, participants live and work in their sponsoring federation's Israeli twin community. Project Renewal is a unique program which has united thousands of Jews throughout the world in an effort to improve the quality of life in distressed neighborhoods and towns throughout the State of Israel. Volunteers are integrated into their Project Renewal community and work in various capacities to enhance the lives of the residents. During this track the Otzmanikim undertake, very often on their own initiative, work with local residents that includes teaching English, working with the elderly, acting as a "big brother" or "big sister," giving music lessons, or teaching and supervising various sports activities. Furthermore, as all of the Project Renewal areas are active in absorption of new immigrants, a great deal of the participants' time is spent helping them.

Independent Track

At the end of the formal program, Otzmanikim continue their Israel experience by volunteering in their field of interest.

Adoptive Families

In order to broaden contact and personal involvement with Israelis, each participant is paired from the outset of the program with an adoptive Israeli family. Adoptive families come from a variety of backgrounds and are members of, or have been recommended by, the Israeli Forum, an organization whose aim is to strengthen the Israel-Diaspora relationship. Participants are encouraged to spend time with their adoptive families, especially during the holidays and weekends.

What has been the impact of the Otzma Israel Experience? At the conclusion of the fifth year of the program, a follow-up survey was conducted to determine whether changes in Jewish identity and behavior could be explained as a function of this particular Israel Experience. The results of this alumni survey were compared to the results of two other pre and post questionnaires, one given to the participant upon arriving in Israel, and one administered upon completion of the Otzma program.

PARTICIPANTS' BACKGROUND

The data that follow report only on participants and alumni of the first four years of the Otzma program, (data from all nine years have been collected by the author in Israel), who had been back in North America for *at least* one year when the follow-up was conducted in 1992. Sixty-eight percent of all alumni responded to the mail survey. Given the young age and high mobility of this population, the response rate is considered very satisfactory. The sample reflects the demographic profile of the population of alumni from whom the data were drawn.

Review of Personal and Family Background

Who are the Otzma volunteers? During the first four years, 42 percent of the Otzma participants were men and 58 percent women. Their average age of alumi was 25 and most were recent college graduates. All these participants were Jewish by religion and 98 percent had parents who were both Jewish. The participants were mainly from Conservative (40 percent) and Reform (43 percent) Jewish backgrounds. They maintained some connection with the Jewish community in their home town, either through synagogue affiliation, federation membership, or participation in Hillel or some other Jewish campus organization.

Jewish Education

In keeping with the goal of encouraging and developing strong future leadership for the Jewish community, recruitment for the Otzma program is very selective. Still, participants do not share a uniformly intense level of

Jewish schooling. In fact, 16 percent of those chosen had no Jewish schooling whatsoever, while another 21 percent had only attended Sunday school. The bulk of the participants, 46 percent, attended afternoon supplementary school while only 17 percent had attended a Jewish day school. In this respect the Otzma alumni were not very different from the NJPS control group. In the control group, taking Jews by Religion, ages 18 to 29 only, 21 percent reported having had no Jewish schooling, 24 percent had attended Sunday school only, 42 percent afternoon school, and only 13 percent had attended a Jewish day school.

THE ISRAEL VISIT AND JEWISH IDENTITY

What can we learn about the postvisit impact of the Otzma Israel experience on alumni who have returned to North America? Furthermore, how do these findings compare to the cross sectional data presented above?

Two measures of Jewish identification are used in this comparison. The first is a response to the question about the importance of being Jewish, the heart of personal identity. The second is attitude toward intermarriage, or the boundaries of that identity within an open society. Does being Jewish constitute a sole and unambivalent ethnic identity, or is it only one domain within an emergent symbolic ethnicity which facilitates marriage to non-Jews? Outmarriage, as we have seen, establishes sanction through the dual-identity household, which in a sense allows for being both Jewish and non-Jewish at the same time. We will also examine how both of these dimensions are associated, if at all, with the visit to Israel

Is being Jewish important to North American 18-29 year olds? Looking at the NJPS data (Table 67a) we can observe an earlier pattern—namely, that among young Jews who have never visited Israel, less than half are prepared to say that being Jewish is very important to them. Among American Jews in the age group 18-29 who have visited Israel once only, the number prepared to say that being Jewish is very important to them rises to 62 percent. Among Conservative Jews this figure rises from 40 percent to 83 percent. The sample size is problematic at the low end for Orthodox Jews, as none of them fail to visit Israel, and at the high end for Reform Jews, where an insignificant number ever visit more than once. Still, among Reform Jews who have been to Israel only once we find, rather surprisingly, that *only 30 percent place a high degree of importance in being Jewish* compared to the *49* percent of those who have *never visited* Israel before. Israel does not, and perhaps cannot, significantly alter the feelings of Reform Jews. *These findings are problematic.* Whether they primarily reflect the values of Reform Judaism, or the status accorded Reform Judaism in contemporary Israel, they certainly reflect the lack of congruence between the two.

Is this national pattern replicated in the New York area survey data, where Jews, according to Bethamie Horowitz (1993, 1994) and common wisdom argue, are "more Jewish" than the NJPS sample reports. Horowitz writes, "The New York Jewish Population Study showed that New York area Jews are notably more likely to identify themselves as Jewish and to view this as being their religion, not merely their ethnicity or cultural background." The answer, then, appears to be "Yes." Again as seen in table 67b, the general pattern is identical to the one reported above for the NJPS data. Among nonvisitors, 42 percent report that being Jewish is very important to them. Among those who have visited Israel just once, 70 percent provide the same response. Among those who have visited more than once, the rate increases to 78 percent.

Findings similar to the national pattern were elicited from among New York area Conservative and Orthodox Jews. As for New York Reform Jews, an important difference emerges. In the New York study we find that 32 percent of Reform Jews who have never visited Israel at all reported that being Jewish is very important for them compared to 55 percent of those who have visited Israel only once. Among Reform Jews who have visited Israel more than once, this rate inexplicably *drops back to only 30 percent.*

The New York data allow us to ask an additional question not asked in the NJPS: did the respondents participate in an organized educational trip? The significance of this question lies in the fact that an educational trip to Israel represents the most widely accepted policy option available to organized American Jewry. Using the New York data and respondents between the ages of 18 and 29 who have been to Israel only once, it seems at first glance not to make a difference. As high as 70 percent of participants in educational programs regard being Jewish as very important. However, when examining the breakdown by denomination in Table 67b, we see that among Conservative Jews, the presence of an educational program raises the rate from 65 percent to 84 percent. Among Reform Jews such a program raises it from 53 percent to 59 percent. But whether these figures reflect the actual influence of the programs, or the already established opinions of those recruited to these programs, the New York data cannot confirm.

Additional support for the thesis of the positive impact on measures of Jewish identification that derive from the educational trip to Israel has most recently been provided by Israel (1997). Israel's analysis of the Boston 1995 demographic study reveals that participation in an organized educational trip to Israel as a youth is highly related to increased levels of adult Jewish religious practice, organized philanthropic activity, as well as inmarriage rates for Jews under the age of 40.

Fortunately, the effects of an organized educational trip to Israel upon Jewish identity can be explored through the longitudinal data of Otzma participants on the same questions found in Figure 19. This comparison, using visitors and nonvisitors in the 18-29 age bracket, eliminates the cohort effect. Here we see the change in the responses to these questions over time, controlling for the background variable of denomination, as well as previous visits to Israel. For the sake of clarity, we compare only Conservative and Reform respondents. Among all Conservative Otzma respondents the percentage who consider being

Jewish as very important increases from 59 percent at the beginning of the program to 75 percent at the end. Four years later, this rate remained at 75 percent. At the beginning of the program only 27 percent of Reform respondents reported that being Jewish is very important to them, although by the end of the program this number increased to 57 percent, and four years later climbed to 69 percent. When we compare these data with participants who had never been to Israel before Otzma, we find that Conservative respondents move from 33 percent to 50 percent and to 63 percent at the follow-up. Reform first-time participants began at 16 percent, rose to 50 percent by the end of the program, and to 63 percent four years later. Veteran visitors to Israel from both denominations reported the same pattern of impact, although at a higher rate (Table 67c).

Figure 19
Otzma: Longitudinal Change in "Importance of Being Jewish": Comparison of Scores at (1) Beginning, (2) Conclusion of Program and (3) after Follow-up in North America Four Years Later; Controlled by Denomination and Prior Visit to Israel Before Otzma Program

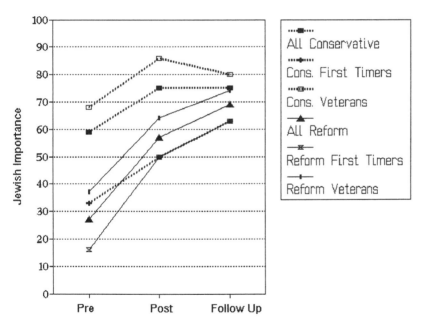

The effect of Otzma on Jewish identity is clear. Unsolicited comments from five years of Otzma alumni convey the tremendous positive impact the program has had on their feelings about being Jewish. Four years after participating in the Otzma program, one alumnus writes, "Otzma was a pivotal program in my ties with Israel and being Jewish. It was the moving Jewish/Israel experience of my life." A first-year Otzma alumnus attributes his experience with Otzma to reinforcing and strengthening his Jewish identity: "Otzma remains one of the best experiences of my life and *certainly* the key to my Jewish identity—or rather the reawakening of my Jewish/Zionist identity." Another comment from a participant of Otzma II illustrates the potential impact of the Israel program: "Otzma created a Jewish identity for me. I grew up where there were no Jews. Going to Israel, the extreme opposite, was an invaluable experience. Since Otzma, Judaism has been present in my day to day life."

The effect of a more standard, tourist-type visit to Israel on the Jewish identity of the participant should never be taken for granted. Still, a long-term visit that takes place within the framework of a quality, intensive educational program has been demonstrated to make a considerable difference over time. Its impact is similar irrespective of one's denominational identity or the degree to which being Jewish is initially deemed important.

Horowitz (1993:60-67) challenges the assumptions of the "head start" school which asserts that the earlier educational experiences are effected—namely, experiences such as bar/bat mitzvah or other elements of Jewish education— the more powerful and lasting they are. She points to the findings of the New York study as proof of the power of such experiences occurring in young adult life. A young adult's personal experiences can be more influential in determining subsequent life choices than the experiences of early or even late school years. "(Having) had college-level or adult Jewish studies, or having traveled to Israel on an organized educational trip seem to have stronger relationship to current Jewish ritual practice than having received formal Jewish education as a child or having become bar or bat mitzvah" (Horowitz, 1993:64). Israel and Mittelberg (1998) have since empirically confirmed the Horowitz challenge, determining that youth whose *first* visit to Israel occurs during *college age* report higher adult scores on measures of Jewish identification than do those whose first visit to Israel was in their teen years. Needless to say, both groups of visitors to Israel scored higher than their peers who had never been to Israel before.

Indeed, Arnold Dashefsky and Alyson Bacon (1994:27), discussing the meaning of Jewish continuity, comment on the bar or bat mitzvah which has come to signify an end to Jewish education for many American Jews. They state that "this milestone . . . has become a tombstone in respect to continuity. A milestone after all is not only a marker at the end of a period but also a stepping stone to a new period in life." For those for whom this traditional life-cycle event has turned out to be a tombstone, the teen and young adult Israel visit can serve as a opportunity for the regeneration of Jewish identification.

It appears that for a significant number of young adults who have participated in an Israel experience program, its impact upon their Jewish identity has been much more significant and longer lasting than the Jewish education they received as children. An Otzma alumnus, commenting on his experience after seven years, writes, "Otzma has had a tremendous impact on my life. The effects were all personal, strengthening my Judaism, reaffirming my values and teaching me more about Israel and the Jewish people than years of Hebrew school alone."

This then is the niche of the young adult Israel experience and the source of its potential transformative power as a second-chance intervention with sociological and psychological consequences. On the basis of the data presented here, it can now be argued that this impact is sustained and maintained at least some years after the participants' return to North America.

OUTMARRIAGE AND THE ISRAEL VISIT

Goldstein reports that a "large proportion of the Jewish population has reconciled itself to the possible or actual marriage of their children to non-Jews" (Goldstein, 1992:128). Among Jews by Religion, only 22 percent would oppose the outmarriage of their children.

An examination of the NJPS data appears to indicate that a visit to Israel is associated with greater opposition to outmarriage throughout the population, including both Conservative and Reform. It appears, though, that more than one visit is associated with a radical increase in opposition, as can be seen in Table 68a. For example, among Conservative Jews, opposition to outmarriage rises from 16 to 19 percent when those who have never visited Israel are compared to those who have visited once only. However, for those who have visited more than once, this figure jumps sharply to 48 percent. Similarly, even among Reform respondents the rate of opposition to outmarriage jumps from 12 percent of those who never visited Israel to 38 percent of those, who visited Israel more than once. One visit evidently makes no positive contribution to the opposition of outmarriage; in fact it drops slightly to 8 percent.

Turning to the New York area data found in Table 68b, significant increments in opposition to outmarriage are found among both younger Conservative and Reform respondents who have visited Israel only once. Among Conservative youth, opposition increases from 27 to 51 percent, with no increment for more than one visit; while among Reform youth it rises from 20 to 38 percent for one visit to Israel. It is important to note that among Reform respondents, for participants who visited Israel more than once, opposition to outmarriage drops from 38 to 24 percent, with a large percentage, 46 percent, maintaining a neutral attitude. One can not help escaping the possibility that the lack of recognized formal status of the Reform movement in Israel contributes to this indifference, but this question cannot be adequately explored further with only the data at hand.

The positive relationship between visiting Israel as part of an educational program and an increased opposition to outmarriage is primarily due to a combination of mutually reinforcing factors. Those who are at risk for outmarriage are exposed to two influencing factors when they visit Israel. First, there is the effect of being immersed in a completely Jewish society—the language, culture, and institutions. Second, and perhaps no less important, is the immersion, in Israel, within American Jewish culture. The total integration with American Jewish peers allows participants the opportunity to evaluate and redefine their own identity as well as their perceptions, including their stereotypes, of other American Jews. In addition, the Israel experience program provides the Jewish young adult the opportunity for an involuntary "singles encounter." This experience unintentionally serves as a mating ground similar to the American university setting or, for Israelis, the army. Furthermore, following a positive experience living in Israeli society as well as among other American Jews, one may seek to connect oneself to the Jewish community upon returning to North America. Once involved in the Jewish community, one will most likely make more Jewish friends and connections, thus expanding their Jewish social network and the probability of meeting a Jewish mate.

Examining the longitudinal data on Otzma found in Figure 20, one observes a rather muted effect of the Israel experience upon the degree of opposition to outmarriage among the overall population of participants. Moreover, changes that are observed between the beginning and the end of the program are often dissipated by the end of the five-year follow-up period. It is worth noting, especially in light of the national and New York data, that quite significant changes are found precisely among the Reform participants of the Otzma program. Opposition to outmarriage grows slightly among Reform participants from 32 percent at the beginning of the program to 38 percent at the end of the program, reaching a high of 54 percent by the follow-up interview. This represents the average of all Otzma alumni. Especially impressive is the radical change among Reform participants who had *never been to Israel before participating in the Otzma program*. Their opposition to intermarriage moved from an original low of *16 percent to 47* percent at the conclusion of the program, and slightly down to 44 percent at the follow up. Among first-time Conservative participants, opposition to outmarriage drops in the follow up study to 36 percent from 47 percent at the beginning of Otzma. This figure is far lower than the 58 percent of Conservative veterans as well as Reform first timers and veterans who were opposed to outmarriage at the end of the program (Table 68c). Clearly the Otzma program had a far more significant impact on attitudes to outmarriage among Reform participants than among Conservative. This is not as surprising as it may seem. For Reform participants, who often join the program with lower measures on items of Jewish identification than their peers, the immersion experience within the Otzma group and Israeli community and society serves to quickly supplement the cognitive and affective dimensions of their Jewish experience beyond what had hitherto been afforded to them. Their Jewish ethnicity becomes far more than symbolic, their spirituality may now be grounded in additional substantive roots.

These findings, which reflect an inconsistency between the NJPS and NYJPS data on the one hand and the Otzma data on the other, highlight another important point which is methodological in nature. I refer of course to the fact

Figure 20
**Otzma: Longitudinal Change in Attitude to Outmarriage: Comparison of
Scores at (1) Beginning, (2) Conclusion of Program and (3) after Follow-up
in North America Four Years Later; Controlled by Denomination and
Prior Visit to Israel Before Otzma Program**

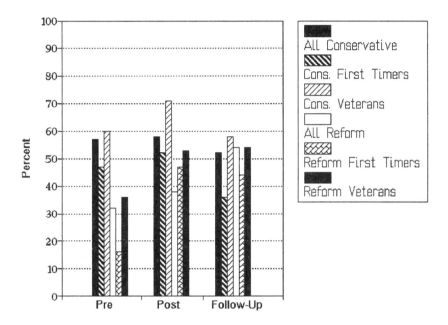

that inferences about the impact on Jewish identity of the visit to Israel are best
based on data that allow the inclusion of the variable of chronological time as
well as the previsit point of origin on the items being measured. Identical
experiences do not necessarily have the same consequences for different
people. The cross-sectional data found in NJPS and NYJPS which stand at the
core of raging community- and university-wide debates on the future of the
Jewish community are simply not sensitive enough on their own to be able to
adequately and reliably assess the impact of interventions that may serve as
possible policy options for community leadership. This is precisely what the
longitudinal Otzma data allow us to do.

One alumna shared her feelings toward intermarriage before and after the
program: "Otzma cemented my commitment to the Jewish community. I intend
only to marry a Jew, which was not the case before I went to Israel." What
stands out throughout this analysis is not a propensity for outmarriage, but
rather a lack of willingness to sanction it. Whether or not to marry another Jew
is simply recognized as a personal choice. Indeed, similar views were found by
Ukeles (1994) in his study of American college students. Most of the students

"expressed a preference for marrying Jewish and the intention of marrying Jewish." At the same time, the characteristically young open-minded and optimistic attitude that "you never know where a relationship will lead" and "love conquers all" prevailed except among the most active of Jewish students (17). This exemplifies the dominant individualistic and libertarian feature of contemporary American society, and likewise American Jewish identity, discussed in chapter four above.

EMOTIONAL ATTACHMENT TO ISRAEL

The relationship between American Jews and Israel is not just based on ideology but on emotion as well. S.M. Cohen (1992a) has found that 40 percent of all American Jews report being very or extremely emotional attached to Israel. The NJPS data reveal that among 18-29 year olds only 30 percent claim to feel the same way. Within this age cohort, 31 percent have visited Israel at least once, making it possible to examine the relationship between a visit to Israel and the level of emotional attachment. The findings are revealing not for the direction of the pattern, but for the steep gradient of change it describes. Among Jews by Religion who have never visited Israel, only 17 percent report a high emotional attachment to Israel. For those who have visited only once the rate rises nearly threefold to 37 percent, while among those who have visited Israel more than once the rate jumps to 71 percent. By contrast, all Otzma alumni irrespective of background and any prior visit report a very high emotional attachment to Israel. Although this feeling may have been strengthened by the Otzma experience, the decision to participate in the Otzma program may also have been the result of it.

The strong attachment to Israel characteristic of Otzma alumni is most probably due to the experience of living and working in Israeli society. In a situation, such as Otzma, where the American-Jewish participant is offered an opportunity to participate as an active member of the local community, it is natural that an exchange of ideas and cultures takes place, and that certain myths are dispelled, all of which tends to strengthen, at least on the microlevel, the Israel-Diaspora relationship. For American Jews who are taught from an early age to feel a connection and a loyalty to the Jewish state, it seems logical to provide a tangible connection to Israeli society which they otherwise would not have. Several unsolicited comments from Otzma alumni reflect the formation of a strong attachment to Israel through their experiences. One remarked, "It has given me . . . a sense of pride about Israel and an insight into the country. I have gone from being very ignorant to feeling very knowledgeable about the current situation and the history of the state of Israel." A third-year Otzma alumnus commented on his immersion into Israeli society: "The program has been an inspiration to me, and I feel the most important aspect of the program is getting to know Israelis—rich, poor, Arab, Jew, Soviet, Ethiopian—that is the experience." Lastly, an Otzma alumna of the first Otzma program writes: "I have a deep love for Israel—a direct result of Otzma. Prior to Otzma (which was my first trip to Israel) I knew next to nothing about Israel and I had no feelings of connection to it."

S.M. Cohen (1991:40-41) has already shown that communal affiliation is positively associated with emotional attachment to Israel. When considering the entire adult Jewish population, common sense might dictate that a visit to Israel is a common behavior among affiliated Jews, since an already high emotional attachment to Israel is reflected in communal affiliation which, in turn, is strengthened by a visit to Israel. Nonetheless, affiliation, as has been reported, is more closely linked to the adult life cycle—the rites of passage of parents and their children. Looking at the 18-29 year olds, where communal affiliation is traditionally lower precisely due to these life-cycle reasons, it is useful to examine the relation between visiting Israel and Jewish communal affiliation. The longitudinal analysis will be found in Figure 21 while the comparison between the NJPS sample and the Otzma alumni is seen in Table 70.

COMMUNAL VOLUNTARY ASSOCIATION AND THE VISIT TO ISRAEL

Goldstein's investigation (1992) shows that 72 percent of all core Jews are not members of any nonsynagogue Jewish organization. This statistic overstates the degree of Jewish disaffiliation from the community. If we look at Jews by Religion we find that despite the low degree of formal institutional affiliation, 79 percent attend synagogue at least once a year, 60 percent make some contribution to Jewish charity, 45 percent say some or most of their close friends are Jewish, and 42 percent live in a very Jewish neighborhood. On the other hand, only 27 percent subscribe to Jewish periodicals and only 21 percent have volunteered for a Jewish organization in the last 12 months. There is clearly some overlap between these measures of affiliation that are reflected in the overall scores on the Jewish Affiliation index.

What is the relationship between Jewish communal affiliation and visits to Israel? The data in Table 31 showed us, not surprisingly, that visiting Israel is more common among affiliated Jews. It is especially strong among those who are formally affiliated and who subscribe to Jewish periodicals. The degree of affiliation also tends to be greater among those who more frequently visit Israel. It is also the case, as seen in Table 32, that this relationship also applies to Jewish young adults who are not yet part of any family or philanthropic-based institutions. It seems fair to say that a visit to Israel is likely both an outcome of affiliation as well as a catalyst for activism and affiliation. Israel may thus serve as an extraterritorial domain of modern Diaspora Jewishness, as well as being an instrument for the recruitment of new members into sparsely populated Jewish institutional life.

Visiting Israel is inherently and unambiguously a matter of personal choice, one which is open to all Jews and non-Jews alike. (This choice, of course, is usually dependent on the ability to cover costs.) It is not exclusive, as the synagogue often is, but inclusive in its structure and opportunities. It can be engaged as an individual, family or a group, and it does not depend for its implementation on advance commitment, even if some would aspire to this outcome.

Is it possible, then, to examine the degree to which Israel does in fact serve as an agent for intensification of community affiliation? Does the Otzma experience have any impact on the degree of the organizational involvement of the alumni? Prior to the program, the participants were asked, "Have you ever offered your services as a volunteer in a Jewish organization before?" Alumni were asked in the follow-up study whether they had done any volunteer work for a Jewish organization in the past twelve months. What we can learn from the data in Table 69 is that there is a significant rise in communal involvement of Otzma alumni compared to their preprogram measures since, while only 38 percent reported having been a Jewish volunteer before the program, a high 76 percent reported such volunteer activity in the alumni follow-up survey (Figure 21). Of special interest is the fact that among the 62 percent who had reported having had no pre-Otzma volunteer experience at all, 73 percent now reported such involvement.

Figure 21
Otzma: Longitudinal Change in the Rate of Volunteering in Jewish Organizations

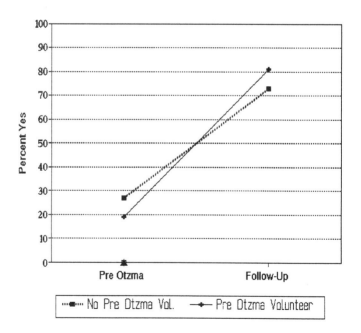

In which areas did Otzma alumni volunteer and how does this compare with their peers from NJPS and NYJPS? It must be stressed that this comparison does not offer us the opportunity for the evaluation of impact but it does serve to broaden our understanding of the areas of Jewish life in which Otzma alumni have become involved.

The data in Table 70 allow us to compare the degree of affiliation between both NJPS youth who have visited Israel and those who have not, as well as between both of these cohorts and Otzma alumni. The key data are found in items 1 and 2. Taking item 1, the rate of volunteering for a Jewish organization, we see that NJPS visitors to Israel volunteer over four times as often as do nonvisitors. Furthermore, about three times as many belong to at least one Jewish organization. Similarly, over 70 percent of all Otzma alumni volunteer in some Jewish organization as well as belong to one.

In item 3 we find that while over 80 percent of Otzma alumni engage in Jewish philanthropy, 68 percent of NJPS visitors to Israel report contributing to (some) charity as compared 37 percent of nonvisitors. Otzma alumni subscribe to Jewish periodicals to a higher degree than NJPS respondents, visitors and nonvisitors alike. Similarly, visitors to Israel (NJPS) and Otzma alumni are more likely to have a majority of Jewish friends, close friends living in Israel and to be living in a Jewish neighborhood.

A significant number of Otzma graduates choose to make a full-time professional commitment to the Jewish community upon returning home. What is so significant here is that many Otzma graduates said that their Otzma experience was the determining factor for choosing a career within the Jewish community. A number of comments from Otzma alumni express the effect that Otzma had on their career choices. Among these are: "I am now a student in the Hornstein program (in Jewish communal service) at Brandeis University. I would never have considered this course of study if it weren't for Otzma." Another graduate commented, "Otzma has definitely been the reason for my choice to work in the Jewish community and to remain committed to Jewish-Israel activities." Finally, "Without any exaggeration I can honestly say that Otzma determined the direction my life will take."

MAKING THE DIFFERENCE

The subtitle of this chapter asked, will visiting Israel make a difference to being Jewish in America in the year 2000? The answer to this question is "Yes" if based on the present findings. The findings suggest that the Israel visit helps to establish a more unambiguous, in contrast to dual, Jewish household identity.

Dual-identity households, generally the result of outmarriage, are the most likely locale for home-centered symbolic ethnicity and symbolic religiosity. In such households the Israel visit might at least serve as an additional symbol or as an agency for restructuring or reintegrating other symbols into a new configuration, thus pointing to the possible connection between visiting Israel and Jewish continuity.

Indeed, a significantly high percentage of respondents who have been to Israel have never had a Christmas tree in their home. Although a higher percentage of respondents who have never observed the Christmas tree custom have visited Israel, a low number of Christmas tree observers have been to Israel. Thus an Israel visit may well contribute to the transformation of symbolic ethnicity and religiosity into a more integrated and coherent meaningful Jewishness or, to put it more plainly, to make being Jewish for modern Americans less ambiguous than otherwise might have been. The transformation, then, is from ambivalent or dualistic households with respect to Jewish identity to households where being Jewish serves as the unambiguous core.

Among young Jews who have never visited Israel, less than half are prepared to say that being Jewish is very important to them. Among those who have visited Israel only once, the *percentage increases by twenty points*. Among Reform Jews there is significant increase in the percentage who, after a visit to Israel, say that being Jewish is very important to them. Yet, *among Reform Jews who have visited Israel more than once,* the percentage *drops back to approximately what it was before the initial visit* occurred. The New York data confirm these findings (insofar as having been to Israel once). Among Conservative and Reform New York Jews whose Israel visit included an educational program, the percent who regard being Jewish as very important is higher than among those who have never been to Israel. In addition, among Conservative and Reform participants in the *Otzma program*, the percentage who report that being Jewish is very important to them *increases significantly* after the program is completed. Moreover, we find that the effect of the Otzma program is maintained years later.

The findings concerning the negative impact on Reform Jews of multiple Israel visits is an enigma. In this chapter it has been consistently reported, both for NJPS and NYJPS, two contradictory findings. For Reform Jews, a single visit to Israel is associated with higher measures of Jewish identification, similarly to Conservative Jews, though from a lower previsit base line. However, multiple visits to Israel, for Reform Jews aged 18-29 only, has the *reverse* effect of a single visit on these very same measures. What does this mean?

In brief, it may reflect the fact that on a first visit, Reform Jews are enhanced by the concretization of the image of Israel, tailored to their touristic expectations. Multiple visits, however, confront Reform Jewry with the mundane reality of everyday life in Israel, which in its present form does not recognize the legitimacy of religious diversity or Jewish religious pluralism. Specifically, this is expressed in the lack of constitutional separation of church from state in Israel as well as the hegemony of the Orthodox religious establishment on the interpretation of Jewish law in the eyes of the state. As is well known from the earlier "Who is a Jew" controversy of the 1980s[1] and the

1998 debate over the Law of Conversion and the Neeman compromise,[2] Israeli rabbinical courts vested with state authority do not recognize religious conversions performed by Reform or Conservative rabbis in Israel and thereby challenge their legitimacy as well as the possible citizenship rights of converts, by virtue of having their conversion challenged by the state bureaucracy.

An attempt to make an historical change in this status quo is laboriously under way through the agency of the government-appointed Neeman commission. Clearly it will be impossible in future years to advocate the visit to Israel as an agent of Jewish identity enhancement if Israel is to be both perceived and then experienced as alien to the core values of America's Jewishness, but most critically, if Israel is seen as obstructing the natural *right of every American Jew to personally choose what that core will include and what it will not.* What this all points out to educators is the need to deal with the interpretation of the Israel Experience after its completion and the recognition that its consequences are never automatic, nor uniform.

Outmarriage is the most powerful factor determining ambivalent Jewish identity. The NJPS data indicate that a visit to Israel is associated with greater opposition to outmarriage throughout the population, but especially among Conservative first-time visitors and all Reform respondents. Why should this be so? The typical young adult visit to Israel involves immersion into a normative Jewish society, being part of a nearly totally American Jewish milieu, and having single encounters only with other Jews. If the Israel experience is a positive one, it is reasonable to expect that there will be a desire to involve oneself both socially and ideologically in Jewish community activities upon returning to North America.

Affiliated Jews, it is known, visit Israel more often than nonaffiliated Jews. Nonetheless, the opposite effect is also measurable. A visit to Israel does increase the participants' level of Jewish communal involvement. For example, NJPS visitors to Israel volunteer four times as often as do nonvisitors and about three times as many belong to at least one Jewish organization. A significant finding is the large portion of Otzma graduates who choose to make a full-time professional commitment upon returning home. The Jewish communal network is ultimately strengthened as we see that both NJPS visitors to Israel and Otzma alumni are more likely to have a majority of Jewish friends and live in a Jewish neighborhood.

From the evidence, it appears that a visit to Israel, particularly a visit that is based upon an educational program, preferably long-term and directed to college-age participants, is likely to significantly strengthen an unambiguous and centrally held Jewish identity. The resulting propensity to oppose outmarriage and the higher degree of Jewish community affiliation among so many visitors suggests a reduction of concern about Jewish continuity at least within this population.

NOTES

1. The "Who is a Jew controversy" refers to the attempt by the Chief Rabbinate of Israel to amend Israel's Law of Return, which guarantees the rights of Jews everywhere to citizenship in Israel, such that it would recognize the conversion to Judaism only by Orthodox rabbis. The consequence of such an attempt in January 1995 (which was ultimately defeated by a 62-51 margin in Israel's Knesset (parliament), if successful, would have been perceived as the symbolic rejection of non Orthodox Jews who themselves represent the vast majority of North American Jews (Hoffman, 1989:216-217).

2. The Neeman compromise proposal refers to the two recommendations by the committee chaired by the then Finance Minister of Israel, Yaacov Neeman, submitted to the Prime Minister of Israel on 22nd of January 1998. These were, first, to establish a joint conversion institute to be run by the three streams of Judaism (Orthodox, Conservative and Reform) to educate prospective converts; second, the establishment of a special Chief Rabbinate court to actually perform the conversions of the alumni of this institute.

CHAPTER 13

Conclusion

MODERNITY, ETHNICITY, AND JEWISH CONTINUITY IN AMERICA

Modern American identity is characterized by a high degree of individualism and freedom of choice. The nature of American society itself is open, pluralistic, and multicultural. Americans, unlike the citizens of most societies, even other Western societies, exercise a substantial degree of personal freedom in choosing, or developing, a self-identity. Americans negotiate their way through the social and economic marketplaces in search of a mate, home, and community.

In chapter 3, ethnicity has been understood as an outcome of macro and micro social forces under the condition of modernity. But wither modernization itself? What are the consequences for culture, ethnicity and identity beyond the commonly recognized modern processes of industrialization, bureaucratization and urbanization? Anthony Giddens (1991:10-34), in a seminal discussion of this question, points to a mode of social organization that separates time and space without the "situatedness of place" (16). Put another way this refers to the integration of people in "lived time" not only in their presence but often, typically, in their absence. This is made possible through the globalization of contemporary life, which has been in turn observed as having the twin consequences of on the one hand, the homogenization of different cultures into one, while on the other hand, the relativization of all cultures, due to the intensive contact between them (Featherstone, 1995:6-10).

More specifically, Featherstone views globalization as "producing a unified and integrated common culture . . . [exemplified by] . . . deregulation of markets and capital flows . . . [which] . . . can be seen to produce a degree of homogenization in procedures, working places organizational culture. . . . Here we find the most striking examples of the effects of time-space compression, as new means of communication effectively make possible simultaneous transactions which sustain 'deterritorialized cultures'." (Featherstone, 1995:115). These forces in turn generate . . . "reactions that seek to rediscover particularity, localism and difference which generate a sense of the limits of the culturally unifying, ordering and integrating projects associated with western modernity . . . globalization produces postmodernism." (114).

If the genesis and persistence of ethnicity has been traditionally understood as a residual outcome of migrant national ancestry and religious affiliation, the dissipation of ethnicity was then anticipated as a function of both generation-time and modernizing secularization. In contrast to this thesis of linear attrition, globalization presents an unanticipated contemporary macro genetic force which generates the invention or reinvention of ethnicity as a response to those very same global forces of cultural homogenization, social meaning deconstruction and the atomization of social relationships that had hitherto implied the dissolution of all ethnicity but the symbolic.

In this world, identity is privatized—an outcome of personal choice. Indeed, the preservation of this personal choice has itself become the metavalue of postmodern society. That is to say, that in the emerging postmodern North America it need not matter what the content of your ethnicity is, rather what matters most is the fact that you can choose which ethnicity to assume when, its intensity and salience at any given time throughout the life cycle.

Hence, the contemporary world becomes one in which the ethnie is not disappearing, rather one where postmoderns typically live through personal multiple identities in a pluralized world. Here Israel may offer North American Jews an experiential edge in the multicultural marketplace of competing ethnicities, but most importantly, the Israel experience is publicly available both to those who seek it as a traditional resource or as a postmodern response to contemporary forces of globalization. Thus somewhat paradoxically, the globalization of the macro categories of cultural identity, may serve to predispose the ethnification and cultural renewal of American Jews through the medium of travel by way of the individual choice to experience Israel.

How may postmoderns accomplish this cultural feat? This is through the construct of the "imagined community". The anthropologist Thomas Eriksen cites his colleague Benedict Anderson as defining the nation as an "imagined community" (Eriksen, 1993:99). Membership in this community is by self-definition rather than by personal acquaintance though what is shared by all members of the community is that . . . "in the minds of each lives the image of their communion" (99-100). Peoplehood then can be seen as forging a connection between a self defined cultural group and a state. In the case discussed in this book however, the unique factor is that the state in question is not the State of permanent residence nor of political citizenship but rather a State of symbolic membership which may well qualify as an imagined community since ". . . it provides a quasi-religious sense of belonging and fellowship which is attached to those who are taken to share a particular symbolic place" Featherstone (1995:108).

The ethnic identity of American Jews can only be understood within this broader global as well as American context. Americans born as Jews have the option of maintaining their inherited ethnicity in the same form, more or less, or of adopting a different form, religious or secular, or none of these. Although, as we have noted, the freedom to choose is not equally distributed throughout society, especially when confronted by boundaries of race, it is less impeded by boundaries of religion, language, and least of all by national ancestry.

Developing and defining one's Jewish identity is, to a large extent, the end product of chosen opportunities and experiences. The range of choices available to the individual are of course not randomly distributed nor arbitrary. In fact, the modern Jew living in North America or in Israel is required, by virtue of modern life, to make ethnic choices on both existential and theoretical levels. The existential choices and the theoretical rationalizations are dynamic and different for Israel and North America: thus the connection between them is as dynamic as it is problematic.

Within the American Jewish community, individual Jews have differential access to Jewish ethnic resources and opportunities, the primary ones being quality Jewish education and the opportunity to visit Israel at a stage where such a visit can have a significant influence on one's identity as a Jew. The filters of differential access seem to be composed of a mixture of socioeconomic power and the commitment to pay the price for ethnic continuity at both personal and community levels.

The structure and content of Jewish identity in America is becoming pluralized beyond the historically familiar. Being Jewish in America today is both a behavioral and normative statement on a multidimensional range of options that are themselves open and overlapping. For the layperson, as well as for the social scientist, a revised typology of Jewishness is required in order to grasp all the modalities of American Jewish expression. These modalities range from the symbolic ethnic option at one end to the separatist Haredi (ultra-Orthodox) Jew at the other. This analysis should also not be restricted to questions of the choice exercised by individuals alone. The issue of household choice of identity is also a crucial issue that requires a deeper and more extended analysis than has been possible here.

Amy Gershenfeld Donella, herself a Jewish-born intermarried lawyer, wrote the following words: "My husband and I, for example, decided before we married that we would raise and educate our children as Jews. We now have four children who celebrate Shabbat, have sederim, build a sukkah every year and belong to a Conservative synagogue. Our children consider themselves to be fully Jewish while recognizing that their father is Catholic. This is as natural to them as my son recognizing that he is male and I am female" (Gershenfeld Donella, 1994:5). Here is a powerful and eloquent presentation of the vitality of the dual-identity household. Yet Gershenfeld Donella is acutely aware that her option is equally contingent on the reciprocity of the wider Jewish society.

She thus closes her article with the following passionate plea: "The continued vitality of Judaism rests as much in your choices as it does in ours" (5).

This poignant example relates the case of an interfaith marriage where both spouses retain their own religion, having decided, a priori, to raise their children as Jews. How representative is this case is difficult to assess. Kosmin and Lachman (1993) point to the rising trend among interfaith families "to integrate the religious festivals of Judaism and Christianity especially Chanukah and Christmas" (248). Indeed, this is the case with many intermarried couples. But what of the next generation? Kosmin and Lachman's data are less optimistic for an unambivalent Jewish future than the possibilities embodied in Gershenfeld Donella's case. In their words, "Among interfaith Christian-Jewish families where both families identify with their own religion, 78 percent celebrate the religious festivals of both religions" (244). These findings corroborate our earlier discussion on the genesis of dual-identity households. Indeed "of the 770,000 children being raised in such households, only 25 percent are being raised as religious Jews" (244).

Thus, Jewish identity, and ultimately Jewish collective continuity, depend not only on the outcome of personal choices and private biographies, though those factors certainly play a role, but also on the way that Jewish institutions at all levels, local and national, respond to the changing ethnic options and opportunities with the openings and closures that they present.

In the search for an institutional basis for Jewish continuity, Jonathan Woocher (1994a) has called for a Jewish community which is multidimensional, comprised of family, Jewish community centers, and synagogues rather than these being only separate "agencies" for Jews. The bottom line is that education for Jewish continuity requires a real Jewish community to be emulated and perpetuated. Woocher seeks to make the public domain of American Jewish life more Jewish and more meaningful for the Jews who live within it.

Sara Lee (1994) wonders under what conditions such a Jewish community is possible in North America today. She argues that the civic structure of the Jewish community and the synagogue world currently operate in a parallel alliance rather than in partnership. What is lacking is the integration of these two domains, at both the macro and micro levels. In her terms, the synagogue world reflects the public space of the private individual. It serves as the collective space in which private life-cycle events are celebrated. In the broader Jewish organizational world, the primary goal is providing services rather than being a basis for Jewish communal life. Lee, therefore, calls for a reconceptualization of the structure and function of Jewish community, which would make the boundary between the public and private domains more porous and require the leadership of both to act in partnership and concert. Recognition of Jewish continuity as an urgent issue on the communal agenda offers an opportunity for reconceptualizing and restructuring the American Jewish community. This issue challenges both sets of leadership to examine the underlying assumptions about being Jewish and the efforts involved in sustaining a viable ethnic community structure in contemporary American society.

The institutional analysis reported earlier prompts us to ask whether the Jewish community should be redefining its goals and *restructuring its institutions* to more suitably pursue the challenges that have recently arisen. This relates to Jewish community institutions at both local and national levels as well as those that facilitate relationships *between* the Jews in the Diaspora and in Israel. In an interview with *Jewish Week* (Schiffrin, D., 1994) Michael Hammer offers a strategy or this type of reengineering. It requires the community to redefine its objectives and make changes in the institutions it utilizes to achieve them. This is not merely a technocratic matter, but an approach requiring interdisciplinary and innovative analysis free of "group think" and "organizational orthodoxy" so that the rebuilding of the Jewish community can benefit both from improved management and renewed vision.

Without denying the traditional obligations of the Torah, the architects of a restructured Jewish community need to base Jewish life not only on transcendent commitments but also on contractual interpersonal relationships. This approach may involve less charisma but may be more binding. One locus for a contract between all Jews could be Israel. Perhaps it is time for a new contract to be developed based on the concept underlying Partnership 2000, which is currently being promoted by leadership from both the Jewish Agency and the Diaspora. Partnership 2000 is a program that serves to foster reciprocal relations between individuals from Jewish communities in the Diaspora and the residents of their twinned regions in Israel. In 1998, 27 peripheral urban and rural communities in Israel were partnered with 110 Jewish communities worldwide. Programs included the development of local lay leadership expected both to promote regional development as well as to enhance the partnership between Israel and the Diaspora through the common concern for Jewish identity. While different public spokespeople are offering slogans and frameworks for reformulating Israel-Diaspora *relations*, it seems that they are begging the question of the institutional basis for Jewish peoplehood of each side from within its community of residence.

This required institutional basis would have to respond to the need to restructure each Jewish community in a way that would add meaning to the present state of Israel-Diaspora relations. The issue is not what new sort of bridge needs to be constructed between the two communities, but rather on the communities themselves. The restructuring must take place *within* each of these Jewish communities so that the relationship between them will be organic, reciprocal, meaningful, and long-lasting. This restructuring might involve transforming the image of Israel from an "overseas" philanthropic allocation into a domestic American Jewish issue. Instead of being a place outside the biographies of American Jews, Israel would become a truly integral part of their lives. At the same time, in a reciprocal and symmetric fashion, Israelis would need to find meaning in daily and regular involvement with Diaspora Jews. They would have to structure a role for Diaspora Jewry qua Diaspora when determining their fate, their welfare, and their Jewish continuity. At present, the average Israeli high school student has little understanding of the character, culture, and structure of contemporary Diaspora Judaism. Young Israelis know more about the Eskimos than about New York Jews and they know more about New York and Los Angeles than about the Jews who live there. Similarly, American Jews (at least those active in Jewish life) know more about Israeli poverty and war than about the more prosaic but truly characteristic attributes of Israeli society and culture.

Amos Oz, one of Israel's foremost authors, spoke to the General Assembly of the Council of Jewish Federations in Denver 1994, about peace between Israel and the other peoples in the region. He said "we make peace not love." Jews in Israel and the Diaspora could also love each other a little less, live in each others image a little less, but develop a contract of cultural and social exchange that would be institutionally interdependent. This exchange could give birth to the basis of Jewish continuity that would offer Jewish content and community to those for whom it is lacking. This type of a social contract, were it to persist over time, could even bring about requited love, but the latter could never serve as a basis for the contract in the first place. Diaspora Jews could diminish their declarations of love for Israel, but recognize its role in their Jewish communities and Jewish identity.

American Jewry, as a population, has moved from one that was primarily immigrant to one that was largely ethnic, to one that is becoming more and more symbolically ethnic. At the same time, this does not necessarily mean that American Jewry will cease to be Jewish altogether. What may be more likely is that an increasing number of young fourth- and fifth-generation American Jews will be Jewish primarily in the mode of symbolic ethnicity, which will permit them to live in comfort in dual-identity households. The questions which remain to be answered are whether such dual-identity households will be able to sustain themselves and sustain the community's Jewish vitality in the next generation, and in what ways will they be Jewish at all.

The question that is indeed being asked, in numerous Commissions on Jewish Continuity in major federations from coast to coast, is to what extent Jewish continuity is possible in North America today? The honest answer is that we don't really know but we can perhaps determine the lines of analysis. We can ask to what degree is the Jewish culture of most American Jews filled with content that determines behavior (often characterized as "ethnic"), or is it reduced to the symbolic? To what degree is this culture—however rich—made plausible to the individuals who share it by virtue of a community structure that reinforces its reality status and maintains processes of socialization both formal and informal, from generation to generation? We can further ask what proportion of American Jewish children grow up in ethnically homogeneous households that serve as the source of the historical memory and culture that is being transmitted to them? By the same token we need to know what sort of ethnic outcome arises from dual-identity households where the adults choose to be ambiguous about their multiple ethnic heritages. In these cases today it is unclear what their children will adopt as their nominal or symbolic ethnicity, if any, and what will be its subsequent strength.

Finally we can ask about the role of Israel in this emerging ethnic culture of choice. Israel is at least the one place in the modern world where Jewish values are nominally those of the dominant culture of society. This situation is in contrast to the minority status of Jewish ethnicity in the Diaspora. Israel, therefore, has the potential for all Diaspora Jews to be a focus (partial or otherwise) of Jewish identification or as a locus of Jewish experience, whether physical or virtual, to be lived through. Denominational polemicists have predicted a narrowing basis of American Judaism, being transformed from a religion plus ethnicity to a religion alone. Since this decline in ethnicity is measured as an outcome of distance from generation of migration (Israel, 1997), its unchallenged objectivity takes on the form of historical inevitability and immutability. Yet this appears one-sided. Israel (1997) and Horowitz (1994) have both shown in separate analyses that younger American Jews today share a set of common background experiences, which I feel can be termed *agents of re-ethnification*. These include formal Jewish education, the celebration of rites of passage such as the bar/bat mitzvah, participation in informal Jewish youth groups, educational trips to Israel at all ages, and Jewish studies courses at universities. All of these separately and together lead us to the conclusion that younger Jews have a more intensive Jewish background than their parents had, especially when considering measures beyond those of religiosity.

One answer to the dilemma facing the young American Jew has recently been articulated powerfully by Phillip Weiss (1996). This article, reflective in the quintessentially modern sense, eloquently argues, perhaps for the first time, that the collective consequence of Jewish discontinuity is both possible and perhaps even desirable. The central theme of the article is a description of American Jewishness as based on marginality—on being the outsider. Thus, the cultural isolation of the Jew and in this case of the Jewish literati ". . . was enormously useful. As a persecuted outsider, I felt superior, motivated and uninvested." But for Weiss this status is now passé and even counterproductive, especially among his "insider" non-Jewish peers, for he reports unlimited access to American society and its cultural resources. Weiss recognizes himself, in fact, as an insider whose outsider status is a lie and is seen as a copout by his closest friends. He affirms that he is a secular symbolic ethnic Jew by choice, building a dual-identity household. Weiss, a novelist and journalist, has read the sociological literature well and knows intimately what he is now prepared to disavow, albeit with some sentimental misgivings but with few regrets. For if the path he himself has chosen in fact leads to a radical reduction in the size of American Jewry, he feels "I can live with my responsibility." This he can do since having defined the tribal culture of American Judaism as essentially an unsatisfying xenophobia that cannot compete with the satisfaction of unlimited individual accomplishment, it remains devoid of any but sentimental positive content. Being Jewish is existentially irrelevant to the life meaning of his being an American.

Israel is mentioned in Weiss's entire wide-ranging article only once, as part of the unholy negative trinity of anti-Semitism, Holocaust, and embattled Israel. It is otherwise apparently irrelevant to his home life—less so than the Christmas tree that he introduced into his home for his wife, and which he reports, earned him his Jewish friend's chastisement. Being Jewish in America is, as Weiss affirms, "an option," but is it an option with any future? Like all modern culture, Jewish continuity is basically precarious. Can we then anticipate the character of Jewish continuity in North America if that continuity is lacking in content, community, family, or Israel? We know that continuity will be even more precarious to the degree it is without content or reduced only to the symbolic which may or may not be a basis for a future generation of American Jews.

The absence of community leaves the American nominal Jew as an individual in a non-Jewish society. Orthodox Jews respond by mandating physical as well as spiritual community. The non-Orthodox and the lesser affiliated who do not share in physical community may, however, build if they choose a virtual community with spiritual consequences. Synagogues, Jewish schools, and philanthropic institutions can all fulfill their primary functions within the realm of virtual reality, for each affords the ability to create a community in time though not in space. Indeed, Israel-Diaspora relations can also not only be observed but partially implemented in the realm of virtual reality. Cultural exchange and personal encounters are already being promoted through the twinning of American Jewish day schools with Israeli schools. This twinning could also include supplementary schools which enroll far more American Jewish children, but for a much smaller segment of their time. Yet in this time it is now possible to intensify their encounter with other American Jews as well as Jewish peers in Israel. Similarly the twinning of communities can be furthered through virtual reality networks, including the pursuit of the dominant philanthropic role of this activity. Dialogues between adults, children, communities, and professional peers can all take place in virtual reality. This interaction is beginning to happen all on its own, it is only a matter of time. *Time* is the quintessential Jewish domain—history, meaning, calendar, celebration are all expressions of Jewish time.

Israel provides relief from the view of Judaism as a minority subculture. The earlier analysis of modern society taught us that the domain of integrated meaning was to be found in the sphere of the private and not the public domain. However, the community sought by the "congregation of institutions" advocated by Woocher can be promoted perhaps if this congregation serves as the *physical* umbrella for emerging American Jewish *virtual* reality. If we honestly look at the sociological processes at work along the broad spectrum of American Jewry, then we must admit that the rapid growth of dual identity households among fourth-generation American Jews threatens American Jewishness as we know it at present.

But what are the prospects of the emerging alternative? In a social world where religion and/or ethnicity are increasingly or *predominantly* home-centered, the ambivalence of the home becomes a cardinal issue. The transformation of the liberal individualist American Jewish culture of the 1980s from being a home-centered though unambivalent non-Christian subculture, into a home-centered but *ambivalent* dualistic symbolic ethnicity is the trend of the millennium's close.

The provision of continuity through the *community of publics*, which is in turn meant to provide the plausibility structure of Jewish meaning for private individuals, *cannot be afforded by the congregation of institutions alone.* Not unless the latter directly confronts the issue of the essentially private domain of home centeredness and the ethnic plurality of that home. In this confrontation American Jews may be afforded the choice of appropriation of a collective memory that is beyond the confines of the domestic here and now. "Beyond" in this context refers both to beyond the physical boundaries of the domicile into the realm of the virtual, as well as beyond the here and now into the retrospective memory of collective history and prospective future—the world of subjective meaning and relevance.

This then is the issue: Can the public congregation of institutions make relevant the meaning of being Jewish to the increasingly home-centered private American Jewish lives? Theology and Israel (separately and together) may both offer the mundane an opportunity for "otherness" only if they are seen as relevant. It is this relevance that the congregation of institutions is bound to provide.

However, the *Israel connection* can be relevant to American Jews, only if the latter are *existentially relevant to Israeli Jews*; currently they are not at all. Thus the American congregation of institutions will be compelled to work with a *grass-roots congregation of Israeli institutions* in order to build together a new common culture that is relevant to Jewish people everywhere.

This is the Israel connection to American Jewish continuity; it is as well, somewhat paradoxically, the American connection to Israeli Jewish continuity. *Jewish peoplehood requires the input of both ends of the assymmetrical though symbiotic relationship* in order to be sustained.

ISRAEL IN AMERICAN JEWISH ETHNICITY

Israel's possible contribution to countering this process of the devolution of American Jewish ethnicity is an additional segment of Jewish identity and another basis for community or Jewish peoplehood through which a Jewish ethnicity which isn't only symbolic may be maintained into future generations. The Israel connection can then be seen to impact American Jewish ethnicity on three levels:

1. *Personal identification—*
   a. Israel as a content segment of Diaspora Jewish education.
   b. Israel as an agent of young adult Jewish resocialization.

2. *Community*—affecting the nature of American Jewish community as a shared element of ethnicity, through effective contact with other Jews.
3. *Israel-Diaspora partnership*—maximizing the day-to-day partnership and common fate and destiny of Jews In North America and Israel, each enhancing thereby the other's Jewishness.

The visit to Israel is a potentially important agent of Jewish ethnicity, precisely because it stands at the interface between the private and the public, the religious and the secular, and the particular and the universalistic aspects of Jewishness. This is a manifestation of Jewish sovereignty which is nonreplicable beyond Israel's borders. Israel contributes affect to Diaspora symbolic ethnicity. It supports Diaspora Jewish identity by acting as the object of organizational efforts in the areas of philanthropy and politics. Ultimately, the effect of the Israel experience is to influence North American Jewish teens and young adults toward Jewish marriage, volunteer social involvement, and communal responsibility. Its normative and behavioral consequences may be termed the *reethnification of American Jews*.

Israel represents a partner for enriching Diaspora Jewish consciousness, for Israel is itself at present involved with its own process of defining Jewish continuity in ways different but no less significant than Diaspora Jewry. Although Israel and Diaspora Jewry have different challenges with regard to Jewish continuity, they need to explore a common and shared solution. This involves a program of reciprocal personal, cultural, and economic interchange between Jews in Israel and the Diaspora. Modern Jewish identity is incomplete without the contribution of both communities. Israelis should seek greater integration of the forms of Jewishness represented in the Diaspora. Diaspora Jewry could develop a better understanding of the historical role and opportunity inherent in the Jewish sovereign state—something that no minority Jewish culture could ever generate. Modern Jewish ethnicity will develop in its fullest form from all that the Jewish people can collectively offer.

MAXIMIZING THE EFFECTIVENESS OF THE ISRAEL VISIT

The results of the 1990 National Jewish Population Survey reveal a positive association among the core Jewish population of North America between a visit to Israel and measures of Jewish identification and Jewish continuity. These measures indicate increased Jewish community affiliation, increased Jewish religious practice, and a lower rate of outmarriage. The positive association between even one visit to Israel and various indices of Jewish continuity persists, even when controlling successively for other variables of Jewish socialization, particularly denomination. These findings are reinforced by the longitudinal data from Project Otzma. The data revealed a change in measures of identity during the ten months of the participants' stay in Israel, as well as in longer terms, as indicated by the follow up study which was conducted more than a year after their return to North America. However, the impact of the

Israel trip, as powerful as its potential, can never be taken for granted. A great deal of attention needs to be paid to the issue of excellence of the program and staff. Furthermore, the importance of a quality educational program, such as Otzma, was seen to be especially relevant for Reform respondents because of the problematic relationship between the State of Israel and Reform Judaism.

On the one hand, it is clear that those who are more affiliated are more likely to visit Israel. On the other hand, on measures of Jewish religious practice and Jewish affiliation, when controlling for Jewish education, age, gender, education, and denomination, respondents who have visited Israel always score higher than respondents who have not. This indicates that a visit to Israel may well serve as an enhancer of Jewish identity for North American Jews and it may affect visitors—irrespective of denomination, age, gender, and region.

There is no prima facie evidence which supports limiting financial subsidies for Israel visits to the very young or teens. In fact, Horowitz's (1993) analysis of the data from the New York Jewish Population Survey reports a significant difference in the degree of commitment to Jewish practice and to the Jewish community when controlling for the age at which key Jewish experiences occurred. Horowitz divides Jewish experiences into two broad categories: (1) involuntary, earlier childhood experiences—formal Jewish education and becoming bar/bat-mitzvah; and (2) voluntary experiences which occur in the teen-age years and on into adulthood. Horowitz's data show a strong positive association between voluntary experiences and higher rates of affiliation and practice *later in life*. The evidence on the influence of voluntary young adult experiences contradicts the approach that the earlier in life Jewish behavior and socialization are stressed, the better.

Israel and Mittelberg (1998), through analysis of the Boston 1995 demographic study, have demonstrated for the first time the importance of the *age of first visit* to Israel and its impact on adult measures of Jewish ethnicity. Their study suggests the importance of increasing the emphasis on college-level Israel educational trips as a key element of the Jewish continuity agenda. Their major finding was that Jews who have taken a first trip to Israel in their college years are more highly engaged in Jewish life, by nearly every standard survey measure, than those who make a first trip at a younger age, and by every measure compared to those who have never traveled to Israel.

These findings, when first reported in a research report for the American Jewish Committee 1994 (Mittleberg, 1994) strongly suggested to community leaders and those proposing the Israel experience as a policy to target a core Jewish population that is single and between the ages of 18 and 29 for a first-time visit to Israel. A high priority for a radical initiative in this area was seen as the precollege or postcollege singles who have never been to Israel. It was argued that this group should be given financial assistance for their trip, since a majority of them are in the low-income-earning category or have low discretionary income and, because lack of resources, constitute a prime obstacle to coming to Israel for the first time. On the other hand, for people who have already been to Israel, income does not seem to constitute as great a problem in determining a return visit.

Another segment of the population identified here are those people in all age categories who have already been to Israel. The data indicate that respondents who have been to Israel report a higher intention on the part of one or more of their household members to visit Israel than do households where the respondent has never visited. Among former visitors, some households report a higher rate of intention of visiting than others. This demonstrates, as S.M. Cohen reports in his Canadian study (1992b), that a visit to Israel has a different impact on different people for different reasons, which includes previsit measures of Jewish education, affiliation, and religious practice. Another segment of the Jewish population which requires attention is young, Reform singles, especially young males. The potential impact of the Israel visit on this portion of the population is extensive, for as the data indicate, they exhibit a higher intention of visiting Israel than has ever been reported or assumed to date.

In summary, there are reasonable empirical grounds to support the assumption that a visit to Israel has some direct positive impact on the Jewish identity and behavior of North American Jews. Moreover, it is effective with college- age youth, which means that a radical intervention at this age could serve to strengthen one generation, both as young adults and as soon-to-become parents. The visit to Israel, and especially the well-crafted Israel experience, provides a window of opportunity. If structurally integrated into the first third of every Jewish American life, rather than into the last third of the lives of a third of America's Jews, it could help bring American Jewry safely into the next century with its ethnic identity intact.

This does not mean that an Israel visit will achieve these goals independent of Jewish education or the Jewish home. On the contrary, an Israel visit only reinforces these dimensions. Indeed an Israel visit adds something unique of its own, the weight of which is not less significant than each of the other factors described. Its independent weight has been demonstrated in the multiple classification analysis above. Thus the visit to Israel neither replaces other aspects of Jewish life, nor should it be used as an excuse for neglecting the other socialization variables. The visit to Israel is accessible to all ages and transcends all historical and denominational cleavages among North American Jews. It is also eminently achievable—its implementation requires the commitment of financial resources in North America and the educational resources of Israel.

These findings would seem to call for a radical initiative by Jewish community leaders which might consist of the following:

1. Determining the prime ages for a visit to Israel. Evidence suggests that directly after high school, the third year of college, and between undergraduate and graduate studies are key periods, the last being optimal.
2. Overcoming financial obstacles by offering a subsidy for all first time intenders to visit Israel in these age cohorts. This would guarantee that all

youth would visit Israel before making critical life choices, such as choosing a spouse, and before making life choices for their children, particularly with regard to Jewish education.

3. Guaranteeing adequate preparation prior to the visit and follow-up of all participants in their first year after the visit in order to maximize the possibility of a second consolidating visit to Israel before marriage.

4. Guaranteeing the quality of the visit to Israel.

Independent qualitative research seems to support this strategy. In the fall of 1993, the American Jewish Committee organized a series of focus groups on college campuses consisting of 155 Jewish students whose Jewish involvement ranged from "active" to "invisible." The purpose of the group interviews was to gain a deeper understanding of Jewish life on campus. Students discussed the salience of their own Jewish identity; the degree of Jewish involvement on campus, including student perceptions of Jewish campus organizations; feelings toward Israel; and the impact of Jewish experiences both prior to and during their college years. The strong impact of a visit to Israel after high school was clear. College-age visits had a "transformative" effect on college students, while family visits which took place at bar mitzvah age and even high school programs had little or no lasting impact among many college students (Ukeles, 1994:14, 20).

There is a very large potential market for such trips. The 1990 National Jewish Population Study calculated that there were 269,000 Core Jews (Jews by Religion and Jews No Religion, in NJPS 1990 terminology) ages 10-14 in 1990. This is the group that in 1998 is of college age—that is, ages 18-22. In 1990, only 19 percent of the current age group had ever been to Israel, but among those who had visited, 41 percent were day school alumni and 4 percent were afternoon school alumni. At the same time, while 55 percent of day school alumni aged 18-22 had visited Israel, only 22 percent of afternoon school and 9 percent of Sunday school alumni had done so. Taken together, these two groups of relatively affiliated young adult American Jews constitute a target cohort population numbering an estimated 158,710 young Jews who have received non- day school Jewish education, but have never been to Israel.

Thus, if the number of Jews currently of college age who take educational trips to Israel can be increased by even only 5 percent, that represents over 13,000 individuals! A realistic though ambitious goal would perhaps be to aim for the 42 percent national average of visitors to Israel, numbering 66,582, but implemented before the age of 29 rather than 92. Furthermore, this market potential will exist for many years, since there are even larger groups of younger Jews, the "baby boom echo" cohorts. For example, the group immediately following the current college-age youth, that is, Core Jews who were 5-9 in 1990 and are now 13-17, is even larger; the 1990 NJPS size estimate for this cohort was 361,300.

If the estimation that between 250,000 and 320,000 Jewish young men and women are enrolled in North American colleges and universities at any one time is reasonably accurate, then a radical initiative would realistically aim at bringing at least 42 percent of this population to Israel for an educational experience visit within the next five years.

The call for a radical initiative made by this author back in 1994, to expand the age range of the target population entitled to financial support for a first visit to Israel to include the college age, has finally found a powerful echo in 1998. In response to an initiative by prominent Jewish philanthropists Mr. Charles Bronfman and Mr. Michael Steinhardt, the Prime Minister of Israel announced at the General Assembly of the Council of Jewish Federations, held in Jerusalem, November 16-20, 1998, the Government of Israel's financial support for the program entitled *Birthright Israel*. The New York Times reported that "Birthright Israel is expected to cost $300 million over five years . . . [B]eginning in the year 2000, Birthright would cover the cost of airfare and the first ten days of a trip to Israel . . . for any Jew in the world between age 15 and 26. . . . There is a wide menu of choices—kibbutz trips, archaeological trips, hiking treks, ecological journeys and historical trips" (Goodstein, 1998:A8). With respect to the question of entitlement, raised by the "Who is a Jew" controversy, the same article reported that "Mr. Steinhardt said he would lean towards 'inclusiveness,' and open the program to any young person 'who chooses to voluntarily associate his or her future with that of the Jewish people.'"

ON THE CONTINUING EVOLUTION OF AMERICAN JEWISH ETHNICITY

This analysis has utilized an open typology to grasp a fluid phenomenon. An open typology does not predetermine the actual forms of ethnicity, but provides the parameters or dimensions that allow us to explain past as well as innovative and emergent forms of contemporary Jewish ethnicity. Its categorization of Jewish identity and behavior allows us to examine the conditions under which this identity is or is not maintained. The mode of contemporary North American Jewish expression has been transformed over time from that of an immigrant ethnicity, to a religious constituent of cultural pluralism, ultimately to symbolic ethnicity residing in a dual-identity household. The issue of Jewish continuity and the nature of symbolic ethnicity needs to be understood not just as a function of the strength and vitality of internal American Jewish communal forces, but also in relation to events and developments within the State of Israel, the surrounding non-Jewish community, and, indeed, the world. All of these modes echo the forces of modernization and its effects. These echoes resonate with the contradiction between the demand for freedom of individual choice, on the one hand, and the simultaneous desire for community, affinity, and belonging, on the other. Being Jewish has become a complicated enterprise, both ideological and social, which requires the multilateral integration of various components into a coherent personality.

American Jews, more than most other Americans, appear to have become increasingly disenchanted by organized religion. As we have seen, their outmarriage level and preference to define themselves as secular, as Kosmin and Lachman have shown (1993:240-245), are higher than those of almost all other ethnic groups in America. If American Jewish ethnicity is to survive across generations, it must move from being exclusively a religion by choice to one that is also a community by choice. It must choose to exist not mainly for the sake of philanthropic, social welfare, and political activities, but as an end unto itself. Its boundaries and network should not be limited to geography, but must include all of Jewish history and Jewish peoplehood.

BEYOND SURVIVALISM—ISRAEL IN THE DIASPORA AND THE DIASPORA IN ISRAEL: CHALLENGES FOR JEWISH PEOPLEHOOD

Yet new days await us. In the days to come, many Jews will settle the land of Israel and our cultural pain will not permit them to remain silent. What is in our day regarded contemptuously—be it due to hard labour or spiritual insensitivity—will cause our successors a profound deprivation of the soul.

As we now grapple with the problems dealing with Hebrew Labour—itself the ultimate question of our very existence in Israel—so shall we grapple in future days with the questions on the fate of our culture.

Berl Katznelson (Pioneer Leader)
In Memoriam of Chaim Nachman Bialik (1945)

The British Chief Rabbi Jonathan Sacks has recently written that "Israel must learn to stop negating the Diaspora. The Diaspora must learn to send Israel its children, teachers and rabbis for formative periods in their development. If the link between them continues to be financial and political, it will wither. If it is educational, it will bloom. In the shift from survival to continuity, the question is less where will Jews live than how and why. A new relationship between Israel and the Diaspora is waiting to be born" (Sacks, 1994: 33).

The segmentation of American Jewish culture, at both existential and theoretical levels, is matched by a sociostructural segmentation of American Jewish community or social space, for it seems that we are experiencing the vertical and horizontal segmentation of American Jewish ethnicity. On the vertical dimension, segmentation is reflected in denomination, socioeconomic status, and Jewish education. On the horizontal dimension, segmentation is expressed through gender, inmarriage and outmarriage, and community. The result can be a segmented identity within a segmented community. In reality all of these dimensions interact with one another, with the results being sometimes strengthening and sometimes undermining Jewish peoplehood. But Jewish continuity requires the maximum integration of all these various dimensions within an overall, worldwide Jewish community.

If we are to apply the insights offered by Arnold Eisen (1992) and of Chief Rabbi Sacks, then horizontally there needs to be a stronger personal connection between Diaspora Jews and the Jews of Israel. This could initially even be developed from a mutual latent symbolic ethnicity, or community of "shared feelings," which in turn could strengthen the attenuation of Jewish identity recognizable in both communities. For while isolated forms of Jewish expression on their own may no longer be able to provide the adequate apparatus for Jewish continuity, the Israel connection may provide not merely an additional and new symbol, but also a vehicle for American Jewish expression that is consonant with America's pluralist and individualistic ethos.

It is perhaps somewhat ironic that in Israel's jubilee year we find that the issue of what makes up being Jewish in Israel, and how that Jewishness determines or affects all the other aspects of Israeli public and private life, stands today at the center of Israel's own quest for identity. This issue challenges, indeeds threatens, in its divisiveness, the very peoplehood without which Israel's existence is unthinkable or even justifiable.

In Israel the time has come to move on to the next stage that Berl Katznelson yearned for over half a century ago, to establish an authentic and indigenous commitment to the creation of a Jewish way of life for the Israeli family and community. A significant part of the Jewish identity crisis in Israel resides in the absence of a sense of belonging, both to the Jewish people and to one's local community. Any serious grappling among Israelis with the issue of *their own* Jewish identity and culture must include a *continuous dialogue with Jewish peers from the Diaspora.* Through this dialogue, Jews in both communities must interrelate so that we may understand and deal with the complexity of Jewish identity—an identity that embodies cultural, national, and religious components.

After a century of Zionism and 50 years of the state during which Israel—Diaspora relations were historically built on the triple negation of the past, of religion, and of the Diaspora itself, contemporary Israeli culture and social life at present simply ignore contemporary Diaspora Jewry and Judaism. This is true in the areas of school curriculum, university studies, political agendas, and so on. Diaspora Judaism must surely become more for Israeli Jewish culture than a distant reservoir of human and fiscal resources for utilization in Israel.

Diaspora Jewry and Judaism need to become one existential focus of Israeli cultural life, which includes the pluralistic celebration of Jewish holidays, marking rites of passage, and interdisciplinary study of shared Jewish texts: for this is an essential and central task of Jewish people building. Jews in Israel and the Diaspora should seek to engage in open dialogue, pluralistic educational endeavors, and shared experiential activities *with and between all of these Jews.* The venue for this activity, both in Israel and the Diaspora, is the community, which serves as the educational setting, as well as the social scaffold, on which to build Jewish life.

Thus the Jewish communities in the Diaspora today could assume a *new* historic role of *partner* with Israel, to ensure the Jewish future of Israel in the Diaspora and the Diaspora in Israel—the Jewish future of the Jewish people. It would pursue this goal by engaging intentionally, purposefully, and programmatically in *Jewish People Building* through lateral Israel-Diaspora Jewish programming, of social engagement and interaction between different Jews from different communities who mean something personal to each other and who live out existential commonalities in partially shared communities, even if only for segments of their daily lives, or at important stages in their biographies. Some successful program examples have already included (1) Israel-Diaspora Twin Community Leadership Development (2) Israel-Diaspora Family Life Cycle Celebration, (3) Israel Experience Peer Encounters.

As Jews enter the next millennium when the largest community in world Jewry will soon be that of the State of Israel, Jewish destiny, private and collective, will be in the hands of the Jewish people as it has never been before—wherever Jews may be. Let no Jewish community be deluded that this is a local victory or a parochial matter. Just as the physical safety of Jews everywhere is linked interdependently, so too is the meaning of being Jewish itself. If there is to be such a meaning, which Jewish children and grandchildren will intuitively understand, it will take the same hard work and immense sacrifice to create, as did the creation of the physical infrastrucrure of the Jewish state and Jewish communities worldwide.

With the palpable onset of peace, or at least the eclipse of the rhetoric of survivalism, comes the inevitable and inexorable demand for fundamental institutional reform in American Jewish life. Internally, the cultural elites recognize and lament the *loss of community*. Externally, Jewish leaders, at both the national and local levels, recognize the *radical loss of membership*. This results in the inability to mobilize the resources that are necessary to maintain the continuity of whatever community may yet evolve.

Hitherto, both groups have utilized in different, though parallel, ways the image of Israel and its needs as an instrument for resource development and community mobilization. Today it is painfully clear that the image of Israel cannot serve as a surrogate for a community that is absent. The challenge to and responsibility of American Jewish elites is to reconstitute the role of Israel in community life by *transforming the image of Israel to an experience of Israel*. They must move the Israel-Diaspora relationship from the *transcendent but ephemeral to the contractual but central*.

Finally, American Jewish Leaders must transform the individual experience of Israel to a community relationship with its own bilateral institutional basis. The next steps beyond Partnership 2000, which is essentially programmatic, is the establishment of concommittant structures, *Regional Israel-Diaspora Federations* which would maintain—along the whole spectrum of twinned local community functions—the intrinsic Israel-Diaspora relationship.

A contract binds two sides. The implication here is for nothing less than the reconstitution of the basis of Jewish peoplehood. At the base of such a contract lies the view that Jewish continuity in Boston and Haifa, for example, is not only dependent on what goes on *within* each community, but also on what goes on *between* each community. While each community can in principle go its own way, the Jewishness of neither will be strengthened by it. Whether this vision can ever be achieved is difficult to assess. However, it is clear that it will be impossible to achieve if the main Jewish institutions in North America and their referents in Israel remain as they are today. The emergent merger of the North American national institutions of the Council of Jewish Federations, representing the local federations, the United Jewish Appeal, which raises funds for overseas Jewish needs and the United Israel Appeal (UIA), which transfers money raised both by the CJF and the UJA to the Jewish Agency for Israel (JAFI), into the UJA Federations of North America, needs to create a mechanism through which they can recast their roles, structures, priorities, and allocations in order to best and most responsibly serve a constituency to which they are hardly known and, therefore, hardly accountable.

With respect to Israel, this need inside America has certainly been recognized. A consensus statement prepared by CJF and UJA leadership in preparation for a consultation on the upcoming merger affirms in its vision statement the goal to "More fully engage the North American Jewish community with Israeli and Diaspora institutions in a continuing effort to strengthen the interrelations of Jewish communities worldwide, and to further a sense of common peoplehood." This vision of creating personal relationships and active involvements between Israelis and North American Jews is also reflected in the declaratory "Covenant Between the Jewish People of North America and Israel", that concluded the convention of the 1998 General Assembly of the Council of Jewish Federations in Jerusalem. Equally important is the recognition by the national institutions inside Israel of Diaspora Jewry and Judaism.

Israel, however, is still a far cry from a consensus statement on the legitimacy of Diaspora Jewry and its potential contribution to the Jewish continuity of Israeli society. In each other's recognition lies the fate of a common future.

With the desired institutional change, or even without it, sooner or later American Jewish leadership will need to radically redirect spending in order to provide for the present needs of the community and in an effort to insure its future. In this enterprise, the Israel connection might play a redemptive role. Like American Jewish identity itself, it is a matter of choice yet to be made. Perhaps this process has already begun.

Tables

Table 1
Israel Experience Youth Programs, World Participation 1966-1993

1966-1969

	1966	1967	1968	1969	4-Year Total
Short-term summer	2,046	3,943	2,689	4,052	12,730
Winter	331	250	221	379	1,181
Long-term	1,072	3,022	1,717	2,243	8,054
Total	3,449	7,215	4,627	6,674	21,965

1970-1979

	1970	1971	1972	1973	1974	1975	1976	1977	1978	1979	10-Year Total
Short-term summer	5,208	8,076	6,396	6,130	5,404	4,457	7,050	10,123	8,853	8,095	69,792
Winter	543	470	498	485	1,829	2,286	2,535	1,225	2,154	2,106	14,131
Long-term	2,383	1,651	1,745	1,669	1,727	1,841	2,205	1,996	1,702	1,657	18,576
Total	8,134	10,197	8,639	8,284	8,960	8,584	11,790	13,344	12,709	11,858	102,499

Table 1 (continued)

1980-1989

	1980	1981	1982	1983	1984	1985	1986	1987	1988	1989	10-Year Total
Short-term summer	6,266	6,308	6,318	7,547	6,787	7,994	6,673	9,251	4,612	5,817	67,573
Winter	1,474	1,754	1,200	2,516	1,947	1,300	2,861	1,640	1,113	1,126	16,931
Long-term	1,193	2,255	2,100	1,690	1,710	2,211	1,941	2,034	1,544	1,455	18,133
Total	8,933	10,317	9,618	11,753	10,444	11,505	11,475	12,925	7,269	8,398	102,637

1990-1993

	1990	1991	1992	1993	4-Year Total	Total 1966-1993	
Short-term summer	5,643	4,163	5,750	6,486	22,042	172,137	66%
Winter	892	1,800	1,350	1,799	5,841	38,084	15%
Long-term	1,270	1,337	1,284	1,306	5,197	49,960	19%
Total	7,805	7,300	8,384	9,591	33,080	260,181	100%

Table 2a
Israel Experience Youth Programs, 1991-1992 North American and World Participation

	North American Participation		World Participation	
	1991	1992	1991	1992
Short-term	2,000	4,339	6,535	7,100
Long-term	1,134	1,515	1,270	1,284
Total	3,134	5,854	7,300	8,384

Table 2b
1991-1992 North American Participation in Post-High School Israel Experience Programs

	1991	1992
Short-term programs (3 - 8 weeks)	206	445
Long-term programs (4 months - 1 year)	419	561
Total	625	1,006

* North American figures do not include the formal university programs. Data collated and compiled by Andrea Cohen from the World Zionist Organization annual reports from 1966 through 1993 and the CRB 1991-1992 North American Participation Data for Israel Experience Youth Programs.

Table 3
Frequency of Jewish Identification of Core Jewish Respondents by Generation

	Jewish by Religion (%)	Ethnic/ Secular (%)	Jew by Choice (%)	Total (%)	All (%)
First generation	84	15	2	100	8
Second generation	90	9	1	100	22
Third generation	82	17	1	100	40
Fourth generation	59	31	10	100	31
All	77	19	4	100	

Unweighted N = 2,061

Table 4
Frequency of Age of Core Jewish Respondents by Generation

Age	18-34 (%)	35-44 (%)	45+ (%)	All (%)
First generation	7	6	10	8
Second generation	5	5	43	22
Third generation	35	52	37	40
Fourth generation	54	37	10	31
Total	100	100	100	
All	33	24	44	100

Unweighted N = 2,056

Table 5
Frequency of Gender of Core Jewish Respondents

Age	18-34 (%)	35-44 (%)	45+ (%)	All (%)
Male	46	49	50	48
Female	54	51	50	52
Total	100	100	100	100

Unweighted N = 2,056

Table 6a
Denomination in Which Respondent Was Raised by Generation

Generation	First (%)	Second (%)	Third (%)	Fourth (%)
Orthodox	46	49	16	5
Conservative	29	34	46	35
Reform	16	11	33	50
Other	9	6	5	10
Total	100	100	100	100
All	7	24	42	27

Unweighted N = 1,799

Table 6b
Current Denomination of Respondent by Generation

Generation	First (%)	Second (%)	Third (%)	Fourth (%)
Orthodox	16	10	2	3
Conservative	34	45	32	23
Reform	23	26	42	40
Other	27	19	24	34
Total	100	100	100	100
All	8	22	40	31

Unweighted N = 2,061

Table 7a
Breakdown of Jewish Identification of Respondents with Two Jewish Parents

All core Jews	76%
Jewish by religion	87%
Ethnic secular	54%

Table 7b
Jewishness of Respondents and Jewish Parentage of Respondents*

	Jewish Parentage of Respondent			
	Mother only (%)	Father only (%)	Both parents (%)	N
A) All Core Jews				
Percentage of outmarried respondents	78	88	32	385
B) Respondents Jewish by Religion Only				
Percentage of outmarried respondents	72	88	27	309
C) Ethnic Secular Respondents				
Percentage of outmarried respondents	100	93	69	55

* Module Sample Only

Table 7c
Jewish Parentage of Respondent by Percent Outmarried

	Respondents Jewish by Religion		Respondents Ethnic Secular	
Jewish Parentage	Jewish Parentage (%)	Outmarried (%)	Jewish Parentage (%)	Outmarried (%)
Mother only	4	72	13	100
Father only	4	88	24	93
Both parents	87	27	55	69
Neither	0	0	4	0
Not asked	5	38	4	100
Total		100		100
Unweighted		N = 309		N = 55

Table 8
Frequency of Jewish Denomination of Core Jewish Respondents

Orthodox	5%
Conservative	32%
Reform	37%
Reconstructionist	1%
"Just Jewish"	8%
Unknown or none	17%
Total	100%

Unweighted sample N = 2,061

Table 9
Frequency of Regional Distribution of Core Jewish Population by Age

Age	18-34 (%)	35-44 (%)	45+ (%)	Total (%)	All (%)
North east	32	22	46	100	43
Mid west	35	26	39	100	11
South	34	21	45	100	23
West	32	28	40	100	23
Total					100

Unweighted N = 2,056

Table 10
Frequency of Jewish Education of Core Jewish Respondents

No Jewish education	34%
Medium Jewish education	43%
High Jewish education	23%
Total	100%

Unweighted N = 2,061

Table 11
Frequency of Educational Attainment of Core Jewish Respondents

High school	21%
B.A.	42%
Post B.A.	22%

Unweighted N = 1,768

Table 12
Frequency of Combined Household Income for 1989 of Core Jewish Respondents

$39,999 or less	44%
$40,000-$79,999	37%
$80,000+	19%
Total	100%

Unweighted N = 1,784

Table 13
Jewish Education by Combined Household Income for 1989 by Age

Age	18-34 (%)			35-44 (%)			45+ (%)		
Income	Lo	Med	Hi	Lo	Med	Hi	Lo	Med	Hi
No Jewish education	45	33	21	32	29	24	37	33	17
Medium Jewish education	30	43	50	48	49	51	45	44	51
High Jewish education	25	24	29	20	26	25	18	23	31
Total	100	100	100	100	100	100	100	100	100
		N = 864			N=507			N = 709	

*Low = $39,999 or less, Med = $40,000-$79,999, Hi = $80,000 or more

Table 14
Visit to Israel by Jewish Identification*

	Jews by Religion (%)	Secular Jews (%)	Jews by Choice (%)	Core Jewish Population (%)
Never visited Israel	69	89	89	74
Visited once only	17	8	10	15
More than once	14	3	1	11
Total	100	100	100	100
All	77	19	4	100

Unweighted Sample: N = 2,045
* Excludes respondents born in Israel

Table 15
Duration of Longest Visit to Israel of all Core Jews by Age

Age	18-34 (%)	35-44 (%)	45+ (%)	All (%)
Less than 2 weeks	9	10	15	12.5
2-3 weeks	23	32	63	46.7
4-7 weeks	27	15	15	18.0
2-8 months	22	25	5	13.3
9-12 months	3	3	1	1.7
A year or more	22	15	2	7.8
Total	100	100	100	100

Unweighted N = 585

Table 16
Duration of Longest Visit: Comparison Between Core Jewish Respondents Who Have Visited Only Once and Those Who Have Visited More Than Once

	One Visit Only (%)	More Than One Visit (%)
Less than 2 weeks	18	7
2-3 weeks	53	41
4-7 weeks	16	22
2-8 months	10	17
9-12 months	0	4
A year or more	3	3
Total	100	100
Unweighted N = 585	N=342	N=243

Table 17
Duration of Longest Visit to Israel by Marital Status

| | Never Married | | Married | |
	All Visitors (%)	Visited Once Only (%)	All Visitors (%)	Visited Once Only (%)
Less than 2 weeks	10	14	12	17
2-3 weeks	25	37	53	56
4-7 weeks	27	27	16	15
2-8 months	20	17	11	9
9-12 months	3	1	1	0
A year or more	15	4	7	3
Total	100	100	100	100
Unweighted	N=119	N=74	N=378	N=213

Table 18
Duration of Longest Visit by Age

| | Visited Only Once | | | Visited More Than Once | | |
	18-34 (%)	35-44 (%)	45+ (%)	18=34 (%)	35-44 (%)	45+ (%)
Less than 2 weeks	3	7	8	15	13	21
2-3 weeks	12	24	59	33	41	67
4-7 weeks	30	19	20	28	13	11
2-8 months	29	24	9	17	27	1
9-12 months	8	5	1	0	1	0
A year or more	18	21	3	7	5	0
Total	100	100	100	100	100	100
Unweighted	N=90	N=74	N=177	N=62	N=47	N=134

Table 19
Visits to Israel by Gender

Visits to Israel	Men (%)	Women (%)	Total (%)	All (%)
Never visited	(48) 73	(52) 74	(100)	74
Visited once	(46) 14	(54) 15	(100)	15
Visited more than once	(53) 13	(47) 11	(100)	11
Total	100	100		
All	(48) 58	(52) 59		100

Unweighted N=2,045

Table 20
Visits to Israel by Age

Visits to Israel/Age	18-34 (%)	35-44 (%)	45-64 (%)	65+ (%)	N (%)
Never visited	79	81	72	60	1,456
Visited once	12	12	17	20	341
Visited more than once	10	8	11	20	243
Total	100	100	100	100	2,040
All	32	24	23	21	

Table 21
Visits to Israel by Age and Region

| | Ages 18-34 | | | |
	Northwest (%)	Midwest (%)	South (%)	West (%)
Never visited	76	75	82	86
Visited once	11	17	11	11
Visited more than once	13	8	7	5
Total	100	100	100	100
Unweighted N's=	291	78	124	129

| | Ages 35-44 | | | |
	Northwest (%)	Midwest (%)	South (%)	West (%)
Never visited	80	91	77	79
Visited once	13	4	10	13
Visited more than once	7	6	13	8
Total	100	100	100	100
Unweighted N's=	253	58	114	126

| | Ages 45+ | | | |
	Northwest (%)	Midwest (%)	South (%)	West (%)
Never visited	69	67	56	70
Visited once	17	16	21	19
Visited more than once	14	17	23	11
Total	100	100	100	100
Unweighted N's=	442	92	178	155

| | All Core Jews | | | |
	Northwest (%)	Midwest (%)	South (%)	West (%)
Never visited	74	76	69	77
Visited once	14	13	16	15
Visited more than once	12	11	15	8
Total	100	100	100	100
All	43	11	23	23
Unweighted N's=	986	228	416	410

Table 22
Visits to Israel by Combined Household Income

Visits to Israel	Under $40,000	$40,000-$79,999	$80,000+	All
	(%)	(%)	(%)	(%)
Never	76	77	69	75
Once	14	14	18	14
More than once	10	9	13	10
Total	100	100	100	
All	44	37	19	100

Unweighted N=1,769

Table 23
Visits to Israel by Combined Household Income in 1989, by Age

18-34

Visits to Israel	Under $40,000	$40,000-$79,999	$80,000+	All
	(%)	(%)	(%)	(%)
Never visited	80	79	69	77
Visited	20	21	31	23
Total	100	100	100	100

Unweighted N=558

35-44

Visits to Israel	Under $40,000	$40,000-$79,999	$80,000+	All
	(%)	(%)	(%)	(%)
Never visited	82	82	76	81
Visited	18	18	24	19
Total	100	100	100	100

Unweighted N=502

45+

Visits to Israel	Under $40,000	$40,000-$79,999	$80,000+	All
	(%)	(%)	(%)	(%)
Never visited	70	69	62	68
Visited	30	31	39	32
Total	100	100	100	100

Unweighted N=705

Table 24
Visits to Israel by Jewish Education

Visits to Israel	No Jewish Education (%)	Low Jewish Education (%)	High Jewish Education (%)	All (%)
Never	82	77	53	74
Once	9	15	23	15
More than once	8	8	24	12
Total	100	100	100	
All	34	43	23	100

Unweighted N=2,045

Table 25
Visits to Israel by Educational Attainment

Visits to Israel	High School (%)	College Graduate (%)	Graduate Degree (%)	All (%)
Never visited	77	77	65	74
Visited once	13	14	18	15
Visited more than once	10	10	17	12
Total	100	100	100	
All	21	42	22	100

Unweighted N=1,756

Table 26
Visits to Israel by Jewish Denomination

Visits to Israel	Orthodox (%)	Conservative (%)	Reform (%)	Other Jewish (%)
Never visited	41	61	77	79
Visited once	26	21	13	15
Visited more than once	34	18	10	6
Total	100	100	100	100
Unweighted N's=	68	391	460	98

Table 27
Visit to Israel by Jewish Identification of Parents

	Mother only Jewish (%)	Father only Jewish (%)	Both Parents Jewish (%)
Never visited Israel	93	95	64
Visited only once	7	3	21
Visited more than once	0	2	15
Total	100	100	100

Unweighted N=301

Table 28
Visit to Israel by Jewish Religious Practice Index

	Never Visited Israel (%)	Visited Once (%)	Visited More than Once (%)	Total (%)	All (%)
Low Jewish practice	25 (94)	5 (4)	4 (2)	100	20
Medium Jewish practice	52 (76)	50 (15)	39 (9)	100	50
High Jewish practice	23 (56)	45 (22)	58 (22)	100	30
Total	100	100	100		100
All	74	15	12		

Unweighted N=2,045

Table 29
Visits to Israel by Measures of Jewish Religious Practice

High Score on Items of Jewish Religious Practice Index	Never Visited Israel (%)	Visited Israel Once (%)	Visited Israel Once + (%)	Total (%)
Synagogue attendance once or more a year	64 (68)	86 (18)	85 (14)	100
Anyone in household attends Passover Seder	75 (69)	91 (17)	94 (14)	100
Anyone in household lights Chanukah candles	69 (69)	87 (17)	89 (14)	100
Anyone in household attends Purim celebration	17 (61)	24 (17)	41 (22)	100
Personally fasts on Yom Kippur	40 (62)	66 (20)	76 (18)	100
Anyone in household lights candles Friday night	30 (59)	51 (20)	66 (21)	100

Unweighted N=2,045

Table 30
Visit to Israel by Degree of Jewish Religious Practice by Age

Age	Low Jewish Practice (%)	Med Jewish Practice (%)	High Jewish Practice (%)	Total (%)	All (%)
18-34					
Never visited Israel	27	57	17	100	79
Visited Israel	2	45	54	100	21
Unweighted N=622					
35-44					
Never visited Israel	25	44	31	100	81
Visited Israel	6	40	55	100	20
Unweighted N=551					
45+					
Never visited Israel	24	54	23	100	66
Visited Israel	5	47	48	100	34
Unweighted N=867					

Table 31
Visits to Israel by Measures of Jewish Communal Affiliation

Items of Jewish Affiliation Index	Never Visited Israel (%)	Visited Israel Once (%)	Visited Israel Once + (%)	Total (%)
Paid subscription to Jewish periodical (yes)	17 (53)	36 (22)	51 (25)	(100)
Affiliation with at least one Jewish organization	20 (52)	43 (23)	60 (25)	(100)
Close friends or family living in Israel (yes)	21 (54)	35 (18)	70 (28)	(100)
At least some or most of closest friends are Jewish	66 (59)	77 (22)	75 (19)	(100)
Live in neighborhood with some or very Jewish character	32 (65)	55 (18)	59 (18)	(100)
Any 1989 household contribution to Jewish charity	43 (62)	69 (20)	82 (19)	(100)

Unweighted N=2,045

Table 32
Visit to Israel by Degree of Jewish Communal Affiliation by Age

Age	Jewish Communal Affiliation				
	Low (%)	Med (%)	High (%)	Total (%)	All (%)
18-34					
Never visited Israel	41	54	5	100	79
Visited Israel	10	60	30	100	21
Unweighted N=622					
35-44					
Never visited Israel	30	60	10	100	81
Visited Israel	14	53	34	100	19
Unweighted N=551					
45+					
Never visited Israel	21	68	11	100	66
Visited Israel	6	52	42	100	34
Unweighted N=867					

Table 33
Visit to Israel by High Jewish Religious Practice by Denomination

	Orthodox	Conservative	Reform	Other Denominations
	(%)	(%)	(%)	(%)
Never visited Israel	38	37	26	10
Visited Israel once	73	55	38	31
Visited Israel more than once	90	69	38	20

Unweighted N=2,045

Table 34
Visit to Israel by High Jewish Communal Affiliation by Denomination

	Orthodox	Conservative	Reform	Other Denominations
	(%)	(%)	(%)	(%)
Never visited Israel	9	15	8	3
Visited Israel once	50	29	25	19
Visited Israel more than once	70	60	39	20

Unweighted N=2,045

Table 35
Jewish Religious Practice by Visit to Israel by Jewish Education of All Core Jewish Respondents

	No Jewish Education		Low Jewish Education		High Jewish Education	
Visit to Israel	Never (%)	Once (%)	Never (%)	Once (%)	Never (%)	Once (%)
Jewish Religious Practice Low	39	10	19	4	12	5
Medium	45	77	58	49	52	38
High	16	13	23	47	36	57
Total	100	100	100	100	100	100
All	90	10	84	16	70	30

Unweighted N=2,045

Table 36
Jewish Religious Practice by Visit to Israel by Jewish Education for Conservative Respondents

Visit to Israel	No Jewish Education		Low Jewish Education		High Jewish Education	
	Never (%)	Once (%)	Never (%)	Once (%)	Never (%)	Once (%)
Jewish Religious Practice						
Low	20	0	11	0	6	4
Medium	51	59	52	41	47	38
High	29	41	37	59	47	58
Total	100	100	100	100	100	100
All	84	16	80	20	62	38
Unweighted N's=		130		245		182

Table 37
Jewish Religious Practice by Visit to Israel by Jewish Education for Reform Respondents

Visit to Israel	No Jewish Education		Low Jewish Education		High Jewish Education	
	Never (%)	Once (%)	Never (%)	Once (%)	Never (%)	Once (%)
Jewish Religious Practice						
Low	14	0	12	3	5	0
Medium	63	77	64	58	60	37
High	23	23	24	38	35	63
Total	100	100	100	100	100	100
All	88	12	85	15	86	14
Unweighted N's=	197		406		133	

Table 38
Frequency of Outmarriage by Age of Respondent

Jewish Identity of Spouse	18-34 (%)	35-44 (%)	45+ (%)	All (%)
Jewish by religion	31	39	69	52
Ethnic/secular	10	6	6	7
Gentile	5	50	21	36
Jewish by choice	5	5	3	4
Total	100	100	100	
All	21	28	50	100
Unweighted N=1,194	251	383	560	1,194

Table 39
Jewish Identification of Spouse by Gender of Respondent

	Respondent's Gender		
Jewish Identity of Spouse	Male (%)	Female (%)	All (%)
Jewish by religion	50	55	53
Ethnic/secular	7	7	7
Gentile	37	35	36
Jewish by choice	5	3	4
Total	100	100	
All	49	51	100
Unweighted N=1,197			

Table 40
Jewish Identification of Spouse of Core Jewish Respondent by Visit to Israel

Jewish Identity of Spouse	Never Visited (%)	Visited (%)	All (%)
Jewish by religion	43	75	52
Ethnic/secular	8	4	7
Gentile	44	15	37
Jewish by choice	4	6	4
Total	100	100	
All	72	28	100

Unweighted N=1,185

Table 41
Frequency of Outmarriage by Age and by Visit to Israel

	Rate of Outmarriage of Respondents Who Have Never Visited Israel	Age Distribution (%)	Rate of Outmarriage of Respondents Who Have Visited Israel (%)	Age Distribution (%)
18-34	62	(24)	19	(14)
35-44	53	(31)	39	(22)
45+	30	(45)	7	(65)
All	45	(100)	15	(100)
Unweighted N's =		351		56

Table 42
Visit to Israel by Jewish Identification of Spouse by Generation of Respondent

	First Generation		Second Generation		Third Generation		Fourth Generation	
	Never Visited	Visited	Never Visited	Visited	Never Visited	Visited	Never Visited	Visited
	(%)	(%)	(%)	(%)	(%)	(%)	(%)	(%)
Jewish by religion	71	84	70	91	36	65	32	49
Ethnic/secular	6	6	7	3	8	1	10	12
Gentile	23	5	23	5	50	22	54	36
Jew by choice	0	5	1	2	5	11	4	4
Total	100	100	100	100	100	100	100	100
All	4	16	20	36	46	35	30	13

Unweighted N=1,185
(All generations: Jewish by religion 53%, ethnic/secular 7%, Gentile 36%, Jew by choice 4%)

Table 43
Visit to Israel by Jewish Identification of Spouse by Gender of Respondent

Jewish Identification of Spouse	Male Respondents Only		
	Never Visited (%)	Visited Once (%)	Visited More Than Once (%)
Jewish by religion	39	72	83
Secular Jew	9	3	5
Jew by choice	5	7	5
Gentile	48	19	7
Total	100	100	100

Unweighted N=589

Jewish Identification of Spouse	Female Respondents Only		
	Never Visited (%)	Visited Once (%)	Visited More Than Once (%)
Jewish by religion	47	68	82
Secular Jew	8	7	0
Jew by choice	2	4	7
Gentile	42	21	11
Total	100	100	100

Unweighted N=596

Table 44a
Frequency of Outmarriage by Visit to Israel by Current Denomination

	Never Visited (%)	Visited Once (%)	Visited More Than Once (%)	All (%)	Unwtd. N
Orthodox	20	0	0	8	68
Conservative	31	9	6	22	391
Reform	40	28	17	36	460
Other	67		54	64	168

Table 44b
Frequency of Outmarriage by Visit to Israel by Denomination Raised

	Never Visited (%)	Visited Once (%)	Visited More Than Once (%)	All (%)	N
Orthodox	27	7	2	17	134
Conservative	40	23	11	34	423
Reform	55	28	27	50	307

Table 45
Frequency of Outmarriage of Core Respondents by Jewish Education by Visit to Israel

	Never Visited (%)	Visited Israel (%)	All (%)	N
No Jewish education	48	14	42	125
Low Jewish education	43	21	38	210
High Jewish education	41	10	27	73

Table 46
The Frequency of Outmarriage of Core Jewish Respondents 45 and Over, Visit to Israel and Jewish Education

	Frequency of Outmarriage	
	Never Visited (%)	Visited Israel (%)
No Jewish education	29	3
Low Jewish education	27	11
High Jewish education	39	4
All	30	6

Unweighted N=557

Table 47
The Frequency of Outmarriage of Core Jewish Respondents 18-44, by Jewish Education by Visit to Israel

| | Frequency of Outmarriage | |
	Never Visited (%)	Visited Israel (%)
No Jewish education	62	62
Low Jewish education	58	42
High Jewish education	44	17
Unweighted N=625		

Table 48
Household Intention to Visit Israel by Respondent's Past Visit by Jewish Identification

| | **Respondent Never Visited Israel** | | |
	Jewish by Religion (%)	Ethnic/Secular (%)	Jewish by Choice (%)
Intend to visit	22	8	45
No intention	68	90	55
Don't know	10	2	0
Total	100	100	100
All	68	25	7
Unweighted N=364			

| | **Respondent Ever Visited Israel** | | |
	Jewish by Religion (%)	Ethnic/Secular (%)	Jewish by Choice (%)
Intend to visit	42	0	***
No intention	45	89	***
Don't know	13	11	***
Total	100	100	***
All	94	5	***
Unweighted N=204	*** N too small for analysis		

Table 49

Household Intention to Visit Israel by Respondent's Past Visit by Denomination of Respondent

Intend to Visit	Never Visited					Ever Visited				
	Orth. (%)	Cons. (%)	Refo. (%)	Oth. (%)	All (%)	Orth. (%)	Cons. (%)	Refo. (%)	Oth. (%)	All (%)
Intend to visit	50	20	26	22	25	88	36	39	11	29
No intention	50	74	65	75	68	12	45	52	76	58
Don't know	0	6	9	3	7	0	19	9	13	12
Total	100	100	100	100	100	100	100	100	100	
All	4	29	55	12	100	11	51	32	6	100

Unweighted Sample: N=364 (never visited)   N=204 (visited)

Table 50
Household Intention to Visit Israel by Respondent's Past Visits by
Respondent's Jewish Education

Jewish Education	Never Visited		Ever Visited	
	Do Intend (%)	Don't Intend (%)	Do Intend (%)	Don't Intend (%)
No Jewish education	13	39	11	12
Low Jewish education	65	44	40	52
High Jewish education	22	15	49	36
Total	100	100	100	100
All	21	72	41	46

Unweighted sample N=364 (never visited) 204 (ever visited)

Table 51
Household Intention to Visit Israel by Past Visit by Age
Member of Household Never Visited

Household Intention to Visit/Age	Yes (%)	No (%)	Don't know (%)	Total (%)
18-34	18	76	6	100
35-44	14	82	4	100
45+	27	62	11	100
All	21	72	7	100
Member of Household Ever Visited				
Household Intention to Visit/Age	Yes (%)	No (%)	Don't know (%)	Total (%)
18-34	51	40	9	100
35-44	44	47	9	100
45+	36	49	15	100
All	42	46	12	100

Unweighted sample: N=362 (never visited)   204 (ever visited)

Table 52
Household Intention to Visit Israel by Respondent's Past Visits by Marital Status

Marital Status	Never Visited		Ever Visited	
	Do Intend (%)	Don't Intend (%)	Do Intend (%)	Don't Intend (%)
Married	19	75	40	45
Never married	26	63	43	48
Divorced	21	76	55	44
Separated	21	79	38	62
Widowed	17	37	39	48

Unweighted N=364 (never visited)   204 (ever visited)

Table 53
Household Intention to Visit Israel by Respondent's Past Visit to Israel by Region

Region	Never Visited					Ever Visited				
	Intention					Intention				
	Do	Don't	Don't know	Total	All	Do	Don't	Don't know	Total	All
	(%)	(%)	(%)	(%)	(%)	(%)	(%)	(%)	(%)	(%)
North-east	21	70	10	100	40	41	44	14	100	48
Mid-west	14	84	2	100	11	34	57	9	100	9
South	25	68	7	100	25	43	47	10	100	25
West	18	76	6	100	24	39	45	16	100	18
All	20	72	7		100	41	46	13		100

Unweighted Sample: N=364 (never visited)   N=204 (ever visited)

Table 54
Household Intention to Visit Israel by Respondent's Past Visit to Israel by Household Income

Household Income	Never Visited					Ever Visited				
	Intention					Intention				
	Do	Don't	Don't know	Total	All	Do	Don't	Don't know	Total	All
	(%)	(%)	(%)	(%)	(%)	(%)	(%)	(%)	(%)	(%)
$39,999 and less	16	82	2	100	44	51	45	4	100	42
$40,000-79,999	19	73	8	100	39	50	40	10	100	35
$80,000	33	62	5	100	17	22	55	23	100	23
All	20	75	5		100	44	45	10		100

Unweighted Sample: N=317 (never visited)   N=169 (ever visited)

Table 55
Intention to Visit Israel by Jewish Religious Practice

	Anyone in Respondent's Household Intends to Visit		
Respondent's Degree of Jewish Religious Practice	Never Visited (%)	Visited Once (%)	Visited More Than Once (%)
Low	9	0	1
Medium	61	26	38
High	30	74	61
Total	100	100	100
All	60	20	30

Unweighted N=160

	No One in Respondent's Household Intends to Visit		
Respondent's Degree of Jewish Religious Practice	Never Visited (%)	Visited Once (%)	Visited More Than Once (%)
Low	30	9	0
Medium	53	52	57
High	17	39	43
Total	100	100	100
All	76	18	6

Unweighted N=363

Table 56
Intention to Visit Israel by Jewish Communal Affiliation

	Anyone in Respondent's Household Intends to Visit		
Respondent's Degree of Jewish Communal Affiliation	Never Visited	Visited Once	Visited More Than Once
	(%)	(%)	(%)
Low	11	10	0
Medium	55	39	27
High	34	51	73
Total	100	100	100
All	50	20	30

Unweighted N=160

	No One in Respondent's Household Intends to Visit		
Respondent's Degree of Jewish Communal Affiliation	Never Visited	Visited Once	Visited More Than Once
	(%)	(%)	(%)
Low	43	17	10
Medium	48	45	41
High	9	38	48
Total	100	100	100
All	76	18	6

Unweighted N=363

Table 57
Jewish Religious Practice by Visit to Israel (All Core Jews) — Multiple
Classification Analysis *by* **Jewish Religious Practice Index, Visit to Israel,**
Jewish Education Index, Jewish Denominations for Respondent, Age,
Outmarriage Status of Respondent *with* **Educational Attainment,**
Household Income for 1989, Gender, Grand Mean = .62

Variable and Category	1	2 Unadjusted	3	4 Adjusted for Independents	5	6 Adjusted for Independents and Covariates	7
	N	Dev'n	Eta	Dev'n	Beta	Dev'n	Beta
Visit to Israel							
1. Never visited	877	-.05		-.03		-.02	
2. Visited only once	201	.08		.05		.04	
			.28		.17		.15
Jewish Education Index							
1. No Jewish education	263	-.11		-.07		-.07	
2. Low Jewish education	643	-.01		.01		.00	
3. High Jewish education	320	.10		.05		.05	
			.27		.15		.16
Denomination							
1. Conservative	460	.08		.06		.06	
2. Orthodox	70	.18		.10		.11	
3. Reform	565	-.03		-.01		-.02	
4. Just Jewish	131	-.24		-.19		-.19	
			.38		.27		.28
Age							
1. 18-34	301	-.02		.03		.02	
2. 35-44	369	.02		.04		.03	
3. 45 and older	556	-.01		-.04		-.03	
			.06		.14		.11
Outmarriage Status							
1. Never married	206	-.05		-.07		-.06	
2. Married to Jew	518	.09		.07		.07	
3. Divorced/ Sep/ Widowed	251	-.02		.00		.00	
4. Married to Non-Jew	251	-.13		-.09		-.09	
			.30		.25		.24
Multiple R squared				.268		.286	
Multiple R				.517		.535	

Table 58
**Jewish Affiliation and Visit to Israel (All Core Jews) — Multiple
Classification Analysis *by* Jewish Affiliation, Visit to Israel, Jewish
Education Index, Jewish Denominations for Respondent, Age, Outmarriage
Status of Respondent *with* Educational Attainment, Household Income for
1989, Gender, Grand Mean = .39**

	1	2	3	4	5	6	7
Variable and Category		Unadjusted		Adjusted for Independents		Adjusted for Independents and Covariates	
	N	Dev'n	Eta	Dev'n	Beta	Dev'n	Beta
Visit to Israel							
1. Never visited	877	-.07		-.05		-.04	
2. Visited only once	201	.13		.08		.08	
3. Visited more than once	148	.25		.17		.16	
			.41		.28		.26
Jewish Education Index							
1. No Jewish education	263	-.08		-.05		-.05	
2. Low Jewish education	643	-.02		.00		.00	
3. High Jewish education	320	.10		.04		.05	
			.22		.11		.11
Denomination							
1. Conservative	460	.08		.04		.04	
2. Orthodox	70	.24		.13		.15	
3. Reform	565	-.06		-.03		-.04	
4. Just Jewish	131	-.13		-.07		-.06	
			.32		.17		.18
Age							
1. 18-34	301	-.10		-.06		-.06	
2. 35-44	369	-.02		-.02		-.03	
3. 45 and older	556	.08		.04		-.05	
			.26		.15		.16
Outmarriage Status							
1. Never married	206	-.08		-.04		-.03	
2. Married to Jew	518	.12		.08		.08	
3. Divorced/ Sep/ Widowed	251	.01		-.01		-.01	
			.41		.27		.26
Multiple R squared		.339		.360			
Multiple R		.583		.600			

Table 59
Jewish Religious Practice and Visit to Israel (Core Jews with both Parents Jewish) — Multiple Classification Analysis *by* Jewish Religious Practice Index, Visit to Israel, Jewish Education Index,Jewish Denominations for Respondent, Age, Outmarriage Status of Respondent *with* Educational Attainment, Household Income for 1989, Gender, Grand Mean = .63

	1	2	3	4	5	6	7
Variable and Category		Unadjusted		Adjusted for Inependents		Adjusted for Independents and Covariates	
	N	Dev'n	Eta	Dev'n	Beta	Dev'n	Beta
Visit to Israel							
1. Never visited	208	-.07		-.04		-.04	
2. Visited only once	65	.10		.07		.06	
3. Visited more than once	46	.16		.09		.08	
			.37		.23		.21
Jewish Education Index							
1. No Jewish education	56	-.15		-.09		-.08	
2. Low Jewish education	172	-.01		.01		.01	
3. High Jewish education	91	.10		.04		.04	
			.32		.17		.16
Denomination							
1. Conservative	105	.11		.09		.09	
2. Orthodox	21	.17		.07		.08	
3. Reform	159	-.05		-.02		-.02	
4. Just Jewish	34	-.23		-.19		-.21	
			.43		.33		.34
Age							
1. 18-34	72	.00		.04		.04	
2. 35-44	85	.03		.04		.03	
3. 45 and older	162	-.01		-.04		-.03	
			.06		.15		.12
Outmarriage Status							
1. Never married	55	-.08		-.09		-.08	
2. Married to Jew	126	.09		.06		.06	
3. Divorced/ Sep/Widowed	74	-.01		.01		.00	
4. Married to Non-Jew	64	-.10		-.05		-.06	
			.30		.22		.22
Multiple R squared		.342		.360			
Multiple R		.585		.600			

Table 60
Jewish Affiliation by Visit to Israel (Core Jews Both Parents Jewish) —
Multiple Classification Analysis *by* Jewish Affiliation, Visit to Israel, Jewish
Education Index, Jewish Denominations for Respondent, Age, Outmarriage
Status of Respondent *with* Educational Attainment, Household Income for
1989, Gender, Grand Mean = .41

Variable and Category	N	1 Unadjusted Dev'n	2	3 Eta	4 Adjusted for Independents Dev'n	5 Beta	6 Adjusted for Independents and Covariates Dev'n	7 Beta
Visit to Israel								
1. Never visited	208	-.10			-.06		-.05	
2. Visited only once	65	.13			.07		.06	
3. Visited more than once	46	.27			.17		.16	
				.48		.29		.27
Jewish Education Index								
1. No Jewish education	56	-.09			-.04		-.04	
2. Low Jewish education	172	-.02			.00		.00	
3. High Jewish education	91	.09			.02		.03	
				.21		.06		.07
Denomination								
1. Conservative	105	.12			.07		.08	
2. Orthodox	21	.33			.20		.21	
3. Reform	159	-.09			-.05		-.05	
4. Just Jewish	34	-.15			-.11		-.11	
				.45		.28		.29
Age								
1. 18-34	72	-.11			-.06		-.07	
2. 35-44	85	-.07			-.05		-.06	
3. 45 and older	162	.09			.05		.06	
				.29		.18		.22
Outmarriage Status								
1. Never married	55	-.11			-.03		-.01	
2. Married to Jew	126	.14			.09		.08	
3. Divorced/ Sep/ Widowed	74	.03			-.01		-.01	
4. Married to Non-Jew	64	-.21			-.13		-.13	
				.46		.27		.26
Multiple R squared					.445		.473	
Multiple R					.667		.688	

Table 61a
Respondents Jewish by Religion, by Jewish Religious Practice by Christmas Tree Custom

Jewish Religious Practice Index	All JBR Respondents by Christmas Tree Custom			JBR Respondents with Both Parents Jewish by Christmas Tree Custom		
	Never (%)	Ever (%)	(%)	Never (%)	Ever (%)	(%)
Low	6 (47)	18 (53)	(100)	6 (68)	11 (32)	(100)
Med	49 (65)	67 (35)	(100)	47 (69)	72 (31)	(100)
High	45 (88)	15 (12)	(100)	47 (90)	17 (10)	(100)
	100	100		100	100	
All	(72)	(28)	(100)	(77)	(23)	(100)
	Unweighted N=1,649			Unweighted N=463		

Table 61b
Secular Respondents by Jewish Religious Practice by Christmas Tree Custom

Jewish Religious Practice Index	All Secular Respondents by Christmas Tree Custom			Secular Respondents by Both Parents Jewish by Christmas Tree Custom		
	Never (%)	Ever (%)	(%)	Never (%)	Ever (%)	(%)
Low	48 (20)	63 (80)	(100)	47 (33)	59 (67)	(100)
Med	46 (30)	35 (70)	(100)	49 (44)	38 (56)	(100)
High	6 (50)	2 (50)	(100)	4 (49)	3 (51)	(100)
	100	100		100	100	
All	(25)	(75)	(100)	(38)	(62)	(100)
	Unweighted N=324			Unweighted N=55		

Table 62a
Single and Inmarried Respondents Jewish by Religion: Jewish Religious Practice by Christmas Tree Custom

Jewish Religious Practice Index	Christmas Tree Custom					
	Never	Ever		Never	Ever	
		Singles			Inmarried	
	(%)	(%)	(%)	(%)	(%)	(%)
Low	5 (69)	9 (31)	(100)	4 (64)	21 (36)	(100)
Med	61 (78)	75 (22)	(100)	46 (84)	70 (16)	(100)
High	34 (91)	16 (9)	(100)	50 (98)	9 (2)	(100)
	100	100		100	100	
All	(81)	(19)	(100)	(89)	(11)	(100)
		Unweighted N=342			Unweighted N=679	

Table 62b
Single and Inmarried Secular Respondents: Jewish Religious Practice by Christmas Tree Custom

Jewish Religious Practice Index	Christmas Tree Custom					
	Never	Ever		Never	Ever	
		Singles			Inmarried	
	(%)	(%)	(%)	(%)	(%)	(%)
Low	61 (26)	62 (74)	(100)	44 (32)	54 (68)	(100)
Med	39 (28)	37 (72)	(100)	54 (40)	45 (60)	(100)
High	0 (0)	1 (100)	(100)	2 (58)	1 (42)	(100)
	100	100		100	100	
All	(26)	(74)	(100)	(36)	(64)	(100)
		Unweighted N=55			Unweighted N=70	

Table 63
Jews by Religion Inmarried and Singles Whose Both Parents are Jewish: Jewish Religious Practice by Christmas Tree Custom

	Christmas Tree Custom					
	Never	Ever		Never	Ever	
Custom Tree		Singles			Inmarried	
Custom Jewish Religious Practice Index						
	(%)	(%)	(%)	(%)	(%)	(%)
Low	5 (85)	4 (15)	(100)	5 (100)	0 (0)	(100)
Med	64 (81)	62 (19)	(100)	42 (86)	92 (14)	(100)
High	31 (79)	34 (21)	(100)	53 (99)	8 (1)	(100)
	100	100		100	100	
All	(81)	(19)	(100)	(93)	(7)	(100)
		Unweighted N=94			Unweighted N=194	

Table 64a
Respondents Jewish by Religion by Visit to Israel by Christmas Tree Custom

Christmas Tree	Never Visited (%)	Visited Israel (%)	Total (%)
Never	61 (64)	39 (90)	100
Ever	89 (36)	11 (10)	100
Total	(100)	(100)	
Unweighted N=1,634			

Table 64b
Secular Respondents by Visit to Israel by Christmas Tree Custom

Christmas Tree	Never Visited (%)	Visited Israel (%)	Total (%)	All (%)
Never	83 (23)	17 (39)	100	(25)
Ever	91 (77)	9 (61)	100	(75)
Total	(100)	(100)		(100)

Unweighted N=323

Secular Respondents by Both Parents Jewish by Christmas Tree Custom

Christmas Tree	Never Visited (%)	Visited Israel (%)	Total (%)
Never	79 (35)	21 (57)	100
Ever	90 (65)	10 (43)	100
Total	(100)	(100)	

Unweighted N=55

Table 65
Christmas Tree Observance by Visit to Israel (Jewish by Religion) —
Multiple Classification Analysis *by* Christmas Tree Observance, Visit to
Israel, Jewish Education Index, Jewish Denominations for Respondent,
Age, Outmarriage Status of Respondent *with* Educational Attainment,
Household Income for 1989, Gender, Grand Mean = .41

	1	2	3	4	5	6	7
Variable and Category		Unadjusted		Adjusted for Independents		Adjusted for Independents and Covariates	
	N	Dev'n	Eta	Dev'n	Beta	Dev'n	Beta
Visit to Israel							
1. Never visited	745	.04		.02		.02	
2. Visited only once	186	-.09		-.04		-.04	
3. Visited more than once	143	-.11		-.04		-.04	
			.22		.10		.09
Jewish Education Index							
1. No Jewish education	210	.06		.04		.03	
2. Low Jewish education	559	.00		-.01		-.01	
3. High Jewish education	305	-.04		.00		.00	
			.12		.07		.05
Denomination							
1. Conservative	419	-.05		-.01		-.01	
2. Orthodox	66	-.10		-.02		-.02	
3. Reform	503	.04		.00		.00	
4. Just Jewish	86	.13		.03		.04	
			.21		.04		.05
Age							
1. 18-34	259	.06		.05		.04	
2. 35-44	307	.06		.02		.03	
3. 45 and older	508	-.07		-.03		-.04	
			.23		.12		.13
Outmarriage Status							
1. Never married	187	-.08		-.11		-.10	
2. Married to Jew	469	-.11		-.09		-.09	
3. Divorced/Sep/ Widowed	215	-.06		-.05		-.05	
			.66		.61		.61
Multiple R squared		.461		.468			
Multiple R		.679		.684			

Table 66
Christmas Tree Observance by Visit to Israel (Secular Jews) — Multiple Classification Analysis *by* **Christmas Tree Observance, Visit to Israel, Jewish Education Index, Jewish Denominations for Respondent, Age, Outmarriage Status of Respondent** *with* **Educational Attainment, Household Income for 1989, Gender, Grand Mean = .69**

	1	2	3	4	5	6	7
Variable and Category		Unadjusted			Adjusted for Dependents		Adjusted for Independents and Covariates
	N	Dev'n	Eta	Dev'n	Beta	Dev'n	Beta
Visit to Israel							
1. Never visited	199	.00		-.01		.00	
2. Visited only once	32	-.03		.03		.03	
			.04		.04		.03
Jewish Education Index							
1. No Jewish education	119	.03		.03		.03	
2. Low Jewish education	87	.00		.00		.00	
3. High Jewish education	25	-.14		-.15		-.16	
			.16		.18		.18
Denomination							
1. Conservative	20	-.06		-.05		-.04	
2. Orthodox	1	-.44		-.60		-.57	
3. Reform	28	-.08		-.07		-.08	
4. Just Jewish	41	-.02		-.01		.00	
5. None	141	.03		.03		.03	
			.17		.17		.17
Age							
1. 18-34	73	.05		.04		.05	
2. 35-44	78	.06		.06		.06	
3. 45 and older	80	-.11		-.10		-.10	
			.25		.24		.23
Outmarriage Status							
1. Never married	33	-.02		-.05		-.04	
2. Married to Jew	48	-.05		-.05		-.06	
3. Divorced/ Sep/ Widowed	44	-.13		-.12		-.11	
4. Married to Non-Jew	106	.08		.09		.08	
			.26		.27		.26
Multiple R squared		.184			.191		
Multiple R		.428			.437		

Table 67a

Importance of Being Jewish by Visit to Israel by Denomination — US Jews by Religion (18-29), Percent Very Important

Denomination	Never Visited	Visited Once	Visited More Than Once
	(%)	(%)	(%)
All	46	62	74
Conservative	40	83	77
Orthodox	N.A.	100	100
Reform	49	30	N.A.

Unweighted N=85

Table 67b

Importance of Being Jewish by Visit to Israel by Denomination — New York Jews by Religion (18-29), Percent Very Important

Denomination	Never Visited	Visited Once	Visited More Than Once
	(%)	(%)	(%)
All	42	70	78
Conservative	52	73	71
Orthodox	96	100	96
Reform	32	55	30

Unweighted N=658

Visited Israel Once Only - Participated in Organized Educational Trip to Israel		
	Yes	No
	(%)	(%)
All	71	70
Conservative	84	65
Orthodox	100	100
Reform	59	53

Unweighted N=658

Table 67c

Otzma: Longitudinal Change in Importance of Being Jewish: Comparison of Scores at (1) Beginning, (2) Conclusion of Program, and (3) After Follow-Up in North America Four Years Later — Controlled by Denomination and Prior Visit to Israel Before Otzma Program

	Pre (%)	Post (%)	Follow Up (%)
Conservative			
All	59	75	75
First Timers	33	50	63
Veterans	68	86	80
Reform			
All	27	57	69
First Timers	16	50	63
Veterans	37	64	74

Unweighted N=168

Table 68a

Attitude to Outmarriage by Visit to Israel by Denomination (U.S. Jews by Religion 18-29 NJPS), Percent Opposed or Neutral

	Never Visited (%)	Visited Once (%)	Visited More Than Once (%)
All			
Oppose	12	21	51
Neutral	40	36	28
Conservative			
Oppose	16	19	48
Neutral	43	28	37
Reform			
Oppose	12	8	38
Neutral	40	55	34

Unweighted N=85

Table 68b
Attitude to Outmarriage by Visit to Israel by Denomination (New York Jews by Religion 18-29 NYJPS), Percent Opposed or Neutral

	Never Visited (%)	Visited Once (%)	Visited More Than Once (%)
All			
Oppose	27	53	68
Neutral	39	23	21
Conservative			
Oppose	27	51	49
Neutral	48	25	42
Reform			
Oppose	20	38	24
Neutral	36	41	46

Unweighted N=658

Table 68c
Otzma: Longitudinal Change in Attitude to Outmarriage: Comparison of Scores at (1) Beginning, (2) Conclusion of Program and (3) After Follow-Up in North America Four Years Later — Controlled by Denomination and Prior Visit to Israel Before Otzma Program

	Pre Oppose (%)	Pre Neutral (%)	Post Oppose (%)	Post Neutral (%)	Follow Up Oppose (%)	Follow Up Neutral (%)
All Participants						
All	40	58	47	53	42	47
First timers	49	47	43	57	49	50
Veterans	46	53	50	50	54	45
Conservative						
All	57	43	58	32	52	47
First timers	47	53	52	38	36	64
Veterans	60	40	71	29	58	41
Reform						
All	32	67	38	62	54	46
First timers	16	81	47	53	44	56
Veterans	36	54	53	47	54	46

Unweighted N=168

Table 69
OTZMA :   Longitudinal Change in the Rate of Volunteering in Jewish Organizations — Comparison of Scores at (1) Prior to Otzma, and (2) after Follow-up in North America Four Years Later

		Respondent Ever Volunteered Before Otzma		
		No (%)	Yes (%)	
		(62)	(38)	(100)
Respondent Volunteered	No	27	19	
Past 12 Months	Yes	73	81	
		100	100	N=167

Table 70
The Israel Visit and Measures of Communal Affiliation - Comparison Between Otzma Alumni and NJPS Jews by Religion, Aged 18-29

NJPS N=289   Otzma N=167   Alumni

1. Visit to Israel by Volunteering for Jewish Organization
   Volunteering for Jewish Organization

Never Visited Israel	8%	First Timers	73%
Ever Visited Israel	37%	Veterans	78%

2. Visit to Israel by Affiliation with Jewish Organization Jewish Affiliation

Never Visited Israel	17%	First Timers	70%
Ever Visited Israel	45%	Veterans	76%

3. Visit to Israel by Household Contribution to Jewish Charity Contributed

Never Visited Israel	37%	First Timers	82%
Ever Visited Israel	68%	Veterans	91%

4. Visit to Israel by Paid Subscription to Jewish Periodical Has Paid
   Subscription

Never Visited Israel	14%	First Timers	44%
Ever Visited Israel	26%	Veterans	68%

5. Visit to Israel by Close Friends or Family Living in Israel
   Friends and Family in Israel

Never Visited Israel	21%	First Timers	83%
Ever Visited Israel	64%	Veterans	96%

6. Visit to Israel by Most or All Close Friends are Jewish Close Jewish
   Friends

Never Visited Israel	28%	First Timers	80%
Ever Visited Israel	50%	Veterans	78%

7. Visit to Israel by Living in Neighborhood with Jewish Character
   Lives in Jewish Neighborhood

Never Visited Israel	32%	First Timers	28%
Ever Visited Israel	44%	Veterans	31%

8. Visit to Israel by Importance of Living in a Jewish Neighborhood
   Importance of Jewish Neighborhood

Never Visited Israel	45%	First Timers	71%
Ever Visited Israel	66%	Veterans	74%

Bibliography

Arnow, D. (1994). "Jewish Identity: A Psychologist's View." *Agenda: Jewish Education.* New York: Jewish Education Service of North America.

A Time to Act. The Report of the Commission on Jewish Education in North America. (1991). New York: University Press of America.

Bayme, S. (1994). "Changing Patterns in Israel-Diaspora Relations." New York: The American Jewish Committee Institute on American Jewish-Israeli Relations.

Berger, P.L. (1967). *The Sacred Canopy.* New York: Doubleday.

Berger, P.L. and Luckman, T. (1967). *The Social Construction of Reality.* Ann Arbor: Penguin.

Berger, P., Berger, B., and Kellner, H. (1973). *The Homeless Mind.* London: Penguin.

Bull, A. (1991). *The Economics of Travel and Tourism.* Melbourne: Pitman Publishing.

Chazan, B (1997). "Does the Teen Israel Experience Make a Difference?" New York: Israel Experience Inc.

Cohen, E.H. (1993). "The 1993 North American Summer Israel Experience Participants of the Youth and Hechalutz Dept. Educational Programs. An Evaluation Survey. A Preliminary Report." Submitted to the Youth and Hechalutz Department, JAFI, Jerusalem.

Cohen, E.H. (1995a). "The 1987-1992 Sherut La'am Program Alumni: A Follow-up Survey." Submitted to the Youth and Hechalutz Department, JAFI, Jerusalem.

Cohen, E.H. (1995b). "The Summer 1993 Israel Experience American Alumni: A Follow-up Survey." Submitted to the Youth and Hechalutz Department, JAFI, Jerusalem.

Cohen, E.H. (1998). "The Israel University Experience: A Comprehensive

Research of Visiting Students in Israel (1994-1997)." Submitted to The Council for Higher Education in Israel and the Department for Jewish Zionist Education, JAFI, Jerusalem.

Cohen, R. and Rosen, S. (1992). *Organisational Affiliation of American Jews: A Research Report.* New York: American Jewish Committee.

Cohen, S.M. (1983). *American Modernity and Jewish Identity.* New York: Tavistock

Cohen, S.M. (1986). "Jewish Travel to Israel. Incentives and Inhibitions Among U.S. and Canadian Teenagers." Submitted to the Jewish Education Committee of the Jewish Agency on behalf of Nativ-Policy and Planning Consultants, the Israel Experience Project, Jerusalem. Jewish Education Committee, Publication No. 4.

Cohen, S.M. (1988). *American Assimilation or Jewish Revival.* Bloomington: Indiana University Press.

Cohen, S.M. (1991a). *Content or Continuity? Alternate Bases for Commitment.* The 1989 Survey of American Jews. New York: American Jewish Committee.

Cohen, S.M. (1991b). "Committed Zionists and Curious Tourists: Travel to Israel Among Canadian Jewish Youth." unpublished paper, prepared for the Charles R. Bronfman Foundation, Montreal, Canada.

Cohen, S.M. (1992). *After the Gulf War: American Jews' Attitudes Toward Israel.* The 1991 National Survey of American Jews. New York: American Jewish Committee

Cohen, S.M. (1995a). "Geographic Variations in Participation in Israel Experience Youth Programs." *Journal of Jewish Communal Service,* Winter/Spring.

Cohen, S.M. (1995b). "The Impact of Varieties of Jewish Education Upon Jewish Identity. An Intergenerational Perspective." *Contemporary Jewry,* Vol. 16. Jerusalem: The Hebrew University, The Melton Center for Jewish Education.

Cohen, S. M. and Wall, S. (1994). "Excellence in Youth Trips to Israel." New York: Jewish Education Series of North America and Charles R. Bronfman Foundation.

Dashefsky, A. and Bacon, A. (1994). "Local Continuity Commissions: A Preliminary Assessment." *Agenda: Jewish Education,* Spring: 22-28. Jewish Education Service of North America.

Della Pergola, S. (1972). *Jewish and Mixed Marriages in Milan 1901-1968,* Appendix: Frequency of Mixed Marriages Among Diaspora Jews. Jerusalem: The Hebrew University, The Institute of Contemporary Jewry.

Della Pergola, S. and Rebhun, U. (1994). "Israel-Diaspora Relationships: A First Quantitative Analysis of Social Indicators." Occasional Paper 1994-13, presented at the International Academic Conference "The Six-Day War and Communal Dynamics in the Diaspora." Jerusalem, 1994, 19-21 December.

Donella Gershonfeld, A. (1994). *Metrowest Jewish News*, Sept. 8:5.

Eisen, A. (1992). *A New Role for Israel in American Jewish Identity*. New York: American Jewish Committee.

Eisen, A. (1994). "Rethinking Modern Judaism: Ritual, Commandment, Community." Unpublished paper presented at the Conference on "National and Cultural Variations in Jewish Identity and their Implications for Jewish Education." January 4-7, Jerusalem: The Hebrew University.

Eisenstadt, S.E. (1972). "The Social Condition of the Development of Voluntary Association: A Case Study of Israel." *Journal of Voluntary Action Research*, Vol. 1, No. 3.

Encyclopedia Judaica (1972). Brandeis, Louis D., Vol. 4: 1295-1300 by Freund, P.A. Jerusalem.

Eriksen, T.H. (1993). *Ethnicity and Nationalism: Anthropological Perspectives*. London: Pluto Press.

Feathersone, M. (1995), *Undoing Culture: Globalization, Postmodernism and Identity*. Sage Publications: London.

Feingold, H. (1974). *Zion in America*. New York: Hippocrene Books, Inc.

Gans, H.J. (1979). "Symbolic Ethnicity: The Future of Ethnic Groups and Cultures in America." *Ethnic and Racial Studies*, Vol. 2.

Gans, H.J. (1994). "Symbolic Ethnicity and Symbolic Religiosity. Towards a Comparison of Ethnic and Religious Acculturation." *Ethnic and Racial Studies*, Vol. 17.

Giddens, A. (1991). *Modernity and Self-Identity: Self and Society in the Late Modern Age*. Stanford, CA: Stanford University Press.

Goldberg, J. (1994). "U.S. Jewry Pins its Future on Education." *Jerusalem Report*, October 6, pp. 26-31.

Goldberg, J. and King, E. (eds.) (1993). *Builders and Dreamers: Habonim Labor Zionist Youth Movement in North America*. New York: Herzl Press.

Goldstein, S. (1992). "Profile of American Jewry: Insights from the 1990 National Jewish Population Survey." *American Jewish Yearbook*, Vol. 92.

Goldstein, S. and Goldstein, A. (1996). *Jews on the Move. Implications for Jewish Identity*. Albany: SUNY Press.

Goldstein S. and Kosmin, B. (1992). "Religious and Ethnic Self-Identification in the United States 1989-90: A Case Study of the Jewish Population." *Ethnic Groups*, 9:219-245.

Goodstein, L. (1998). *New York Times*, November 16:A8.

Gross, M.I. (1993). "Paradigms of Jewish Ethnicity: Methodological and Normative Implications." *Jewish Journal of Sociology*, Vol. 35, No. 1.

Grossbard-Shechtman, S. (1993). *On the Economics of Marriage: A Theory of Marriage, Labour and Divorce*, Boulder, CO: Westview Press.

Harman, D. (1993). Foreword to G. Elad, *The Israel Experience. Planning for 1994.* Joint Authority for Jewish Zionist Education. The Charles R.

Bronfman Foundation, Israel.

Hochstein, A. (1986). "The Israel Experience Educational Programs in Israel." Summary Report to the Jewish Education Committee, the Jewish Agency for Israel, Jerusalem.

Hoffman, C. (1989). *The Smoke Screen: Israel, Philanthropy and American Jews*. Silver Spring, Maryland: Eshel Books.

Horowitz, B. (1993). *The 1991 New York Jewish Population Study*. UJA-Federation of Jewish Philanthropies of New York, Inc.

Horowitz, B. (1994). "Jewishness in New York: Exception or Rule?" Unpublished paper presented at Conference on "National and Cultural Variations in Jewish Identity and Their Implications for Jewish Education." January 4-7, Jerusalem: The Hebrew University.

Horowitz, T. and Cialic, M. (1969). *Volunteers for Israel*. Research Report No. 127, publication No. 473, Jerusalem: Henrietta Szold Institute (in association with J. Hodora).

Israel, S. (1997). *Comprehensive Report on the 1995 CJP Demographic Study*. Combined Jewish Philanthropies of Greater Boston.

Israel, S. and Mittelberg, D. (1998). *The Israel Visit—Not Just for Teens: The Characteristics and Impact of College-age Travel to Israel*. Waltham, MA.: Brandeis University, Cohen Center for Modern Jewish Studies.

Kafka, R. and London, P. (1990) Longitudinal Evaluation: Follow-up of Alumni of Israel programs in North America. Cambridge, MA: Harvard University, Project for Kibbutz Studies Newsletter.

Karp, A.J. (1985). *Haven and Home*. New York: Schocken Books.

Kivisto, P. and Nefzger, B. (1993). "Symbolic Ethnicity and American Jews: The Relationship of Ethnic Identity to Behaviour and Group Affiliation." *The Social Science Journal*, Vol. 30, No.1.

Kosmin, B.A., Goldstein, S., Waksberg J., Lerer, N., Keysar, A., and Scheckner, J. (1991). *Highlights of the CJF 1990 National Jewish Population Survey*. New York: Council of Jewish Federations.

Kosmin, B.A. and Lachman, S. (1993). *One Nation Under God*. New York: Harmony Books.

Lee, S. (1994). "Federations, Synagogues and Jewish Continuity." *Agenda: Jewish Education*. Spring: 28-32. Jewish Education Service of North America.

Lieberson, S. (1985). "Unhyphenated Whites in the United States." *Ethnic and Racial Studies*, Vol. 8, No. 1.

Liebler, I. (1994). *The Israel-Diaspora Identity Crisis: A Looming Disaster*. New York: The Institute of the World Jewish Congress.

Masserik, F., and Chenkin, A. (1973). "United States National Jewish Population Study: A First Report." *American Jewish Yearbook*, Vol. 74. Philadelphia: Jewish Publication Society.

Medding, P.Y., Tobin, G.A., Barack Fishman, S., and Rimor, M. (1992). "Jewish Identity in Conversionary and Mixed Marriages." *American Jewish Yearbook*, Vol. 92.

Mittelberg, D. (1988). *Strangers in Paradise: The Israeli Kibbutz Experience.* New Brunswick, NJ: Transaction.

Mittleberg, D. (1990). Longitudinal Evaluation of the Kibbutz Experience: The Case of the Kibbutz Institutes for Jewish Experience. Cambridge, MA.: Harvard University, Project for Kibbutz Studies Newsletter,

Mittelberg, D. (1992). "The Impact of Jewish Education and the 'Israel Experience' on the Jewish Identity of American Jewish Youth." *Studies in Contemporary Jewry*, Vol. 8.

Mittelberg, D. (1994). *The Israel Visit and Jewish Identification.* The Institute on American Jewish Israeli Relations, Issue Series No. 4, American Jewish Committee.

Mittelberg, D. and Lev-Ari, L. (1991). *The Kibbutz as an Educational Setting for Jewish Youth from Abroad.* Haifa: University of Haifa, The University Center of the Kibbutz and the Cooperative Idea.

Mittelberg, D. and Lev-Ari, L. (1995). "Jewish Identity, Jewish Education and Experience of the Kibbutz in Israel." *Journal of Moral Education*, Vol. 24, No. 3.

Mittelberg, D. and Waters, M. (1992). "The Process of Ethnogenesis Among Haitian and Israeli Immigrants in the United States." *Ethnic and Racial Studies*, Vol. 15, No. 3.

Norich, S. (1994). *What Will Bind Us Now? A Report on the Institutional Ties Between Israel and American Jewry.* New York: Center for Middle East Peace and Economic Cooperation.

Reimer, D. (1995). "Jewish Education Takes the Inside Track in the Race to 'Keep 'em Jewish' as Federations Decide Who to Back." *MetroWest*, January 26.

Ritterband, P. (1994). ". . . Only by Virtue of Its Torah." *Agenda: Jewish Education*, Jewish Education Service of North America.

Sacks, J. (1994). "Beyond the Cult of Survival." *Jerusalem Report*, March 10, pp.30-33.

Schifrin, D. (1994). "Radical Redesign." *Jewish Week*, November 11-24.

Shulman, M. (1990). Retrospective Alumni Evaluation of Israel Experience Programs. Cambridge, MA: Harvard University, Project for Kibbutz Studies Newsletter.

Silberman, C. (1985). *A Certain People.* New York: Summit Books.

Slutzki, Y. (1972). "The History of the Haganah." Vol. 3, Part 2: *From Battle to War.* Tel Aviv: Am Oved (Hebrew).

Sobel, Z. (1993). "A Small Place in Galilee: Religion and Social Conflict in an Israeli Village." In *New Perspectives Jewish Life and Thought.* New York: Holmes & Meier.

Spiegel, F.Z. (1994). "One Dose of Israel." *Jerusalem Report*, October 20, p. 54.

Sternberg, L. and Rimor, M. (1990). Hillel Leaders Study: Israel Experience and Jewish Leadership Development. Cambridge, MA: Harvard University, Project for Kibbutz Studies Newsletter.

Streicker, J. and Tobin, G. A. (1995). "Assessment of the Linkages to Israel Program. Waltham, MA: Brandeis University, Maurice and Marilyn Cohen Center for Modern Jewish Studies, Institute for Community and Religion.

Stone, J. (1985). *Racial Conflict in Contemporary Society.* Cambridge, MA: Harvard University Press.

Tobin, G.A. (1990). *Israel and American Jewish Philanthropy.* Policy and Planning Paper 5. Waltham, MA: Brandeis University, Maurice and Marilyn Cohen Center for Modern Jewish Studies, Institute for Community and Religion.

Ukeles, J. (1994). *Campus and Community: Strengthening the Identity of Jewish Collge Students.* New York: American Jewish Committee.

United Jewish Appeal Federation of Jewish Philanthropies of New York, Inc. (1995). "Reinventing the Jewish Agency for the Twenty-First Century." Submitted to the United Israel Appeal and the Goals and Priorities Committee.

Urman, S. (1990). Evaluation of Israel Summer Programs for Canadian Youth. Cambridge, MA: Harvard University, Project for Kibbutz Studies Newsletter.

Waters, M.C. (1990). *Ethnic Options: Choosing Identities in America.* Berkeley: University of California Press.

Waxman, C.I. (1981). "The Fourth Generation Grows Up: The Contemporary American Jewish Community." *Annals*, AAPSS, No. 454.

Waxman, C.I. (1989). *American Aliya: Portrait of an Innovative Migration Movement.* Detroit: Wayne State University Press

Weiss, P. (1996). "Being Jewish." *New York*, January 29: 25-33.

Wiernik, P. (1972). *History of the Jews in America.* New York: Hermon Press.

Woocher, J. (1986). *Sacred Survival: The Civil Religion of American Jews.* Bloomington: Indiana University Press.

Woocher, J. (1994a). "Community and Continuity." *Agenda: Jewish Education,* 16-21. New York: Jewish Education Service of North America, Inc. Issue # 4, Spring 1994.

Woocher, J. (1994b). *Toward a "Unified Field Theory" of Jewish Continuity.* New York: Jewish Education Service of North America, Inc.

Index

About the Author

DAVID MITTELBERG is former head and current research associate at The Institute for Research of the Kibbutz and the Cooperative Idea, Haifa University and Lecturer in Sociology at the Oranim and Jezreel Academic Colleges. Professor Mittelberg has published widely on kibbutz, gender, ethnicity, and migration.